Bloom's Modern Critical Interpretations

Bloom's Modern Critical Interpretations

Bloom's Modern Critical Interpretations

Gabriel García Márquez's
Love in the Time of Cholera

Edited and with an introduction by
Harold Bloom
Sterling Professor of the Humanities
Yale University

CHELSEA HOUSE
PUBLISHERS
A Haights Cross Communications Company

Philadelphia

Printed and bound in the United States of America.
10 9 8 7 6 5 4 3 2 1

Library of Congress Cataloging-in-Publication Data

Gabriel García Márquez's Love in the time of cholera / [edited by] Harold Bloom.
      p. cm. — (Modern critical interpretations)
   Includes bibliographical references and index.
   ISBN 0-7910-8120-6 (alk. paper)
   1. García Márquez, Gabriel, 1928- Amor en los tiempos del cólera. I. Bloom, Harold. II.
Series.
   PQ8180.17.A73A8345 2004
   863'.64—dc22
                                        2004023882

Contributing Editor: Gabriel Welsch and Elizabeth Beaudin

Cover designed by Keith Trego

Cover photo: Library of Congress, LC-USZC2-847

Layout by EJB Publishing Services

Contents

Editor's Note

My Introduction attempts to account for my strong sense that *Love in the Time of Cholera* could be a more lasting work than *One Hundred Years of Solitude* may prove to be.

Rubén Pelayo helps to document the social history of García Márquez's love story, while Roberto González-Echevarría acutely sees that the novel concerns the conflict between eros and society, and thus indicates a connection to *Don Quixote*.

For Gene H. Bell-Villada, García Márquez's purpose is best defined as a reversal of our social disdain for sexuality in old age, after which Michael Bell sees *Cholera* as a popular romance that both invokes the spirit of Flaubert's irony and also takes on Flaubert in a narrative *agon*.

Humanistic hope even in our new darkness is identified as *Cholera's* stance by David Buehrer, while Mabel Moraña celebrates the book's advocacy of heroic individuality.

Jean Franco emphasizes the novel's wedge between private and public good, after which M. Keith Booker centers on the narrative's seductiveness.

A feminist perspective is supplied by Anny Brooksbank Jones, who shrewdly concludes that García Márquez's "feminism" is ambiguous, while Michael Wood eloquently completes this volume by meditating upon different representations of temporality in *Cholera*.

HAROLD BLOOM

Introduction

The aesthetic principle of *Love in the Time of Cholera* is only a slightly chastened version of what might be the motto of *One Hundred Years of Solitude*: "Anything goes," or even "Everything goes." Anything and everything goes into the mix: Faulkner, Kafka, Borges, Carpentier, Conrad, Joyce. Both novels are Scriptures: *Solitude* is an Old Testament, and *Cholera* a *New Testament*, at least for García Márquez and the most devoted of his readers and critics. I myself have come to value *Cholera* over *Solitude*, but that is a choice of riches.

What Faulkner—who most valued the Bible (as literature only), Shakespeare, Melville, Conrad, and Joyce—would have made of these New World Hispanic masterpieces, I cannot surmise. The verbal cascades he would have recognized as akin to his own, and the heroic individualism surely would have moved him. Yet he went about while waiting for his doom to lift, and his greatest figures—Darl Bundren, Quentin Compson, Sutpen, Joe Christmas, Popeye—are damned beyond damnation. Though Faulkner could be as grandly comic as Dickens, as is witnessed by the Snopes family, who now constitute the Texan Republican party, led by Tom DeLay Snopes, while our nation has chosen Benito Bush as Il Duce. Oscar Wilde was always right: life has no choice but to imitate art.

The antic joy of García Márquez might have been shrugged away by Faulkner, at least in his tragic mode, but he would have approved the last-ditch humanism affirmed both by precursor and latecomer. Decadence, the obsessive fear of incest, the drowning out of creative solitude by an ocean of information: these are common themes and apprehensions. What then is the saving difference, besides amazing high spirits in García Márquez, that distinguishes the two?

Faulkner's hopes rarely are persuasive: his greatest characters are as nihilistic as Shakespeare's. The immense popularity of García Márquez was earned by his exuberance, which veils his own apocalyptic forebodings. What Shakespeare was to Faulkner, Cervantes necessarily is to García Márquez: the truest ancestor. Cervantes, in his dark wisdom, is not less nihilistic than Shakespeare, and I do not believe that either ultimately was a Christian believer, any more than Faulkner or García Márquez can be said to be.

García Márquez's difference from all three is more evident in *Cholera* than in *Solitude*: he really does have a High Romantic faith in Eros, though he knows the Freudian truth that love too frequently is a mask for the Death Drive. Yet I prefer *Cholera* to *Solitude* finally because Florentine Ariza is dauntless, as here in the novel's closing passage:

> "Let us keep going, going, going, back to La Dorada."
>
> Fermina Daza shuddered because she recognized his former voice, illuminated by the grace of the Holy Spirit, and she looked at the Captain: he was their destiny. But the Captain did not see her because he was stupefied by Florentino Ariza's tremendous powers of inspiration.
>
> "Do you mean what you say?" he asked.
>
> "From the moment I was born," said Florentino Ariza, "I have never said anything I did not mean."
>
> The Captain looked at Fermina Daza and saw on her eyelashes the first glimmer of wintry frost. Then he looked at Florentino Ariza, his invincible power, his intrepid love, and he was overwhelmed by the belated suspicion that it is life, more than death, that has no limit.
>
> "And how long do you think we can keep up this goddamn coming and going?" he asked.
>
> Florentino Ariza had kept his answer ready for fifty-three years, seven months, and eleven days and nights.
>
> "Forever," he said.

RUBÉN PELAYO

Love in the Time of Cholera

Carlos R. Rodríguez, a friend of García Márquez and well-known literary critic, wrote that if *One Hundred Years of Solitude* had not secured the road to Stockholm for García Márquez to receive the Nobel Prize in literature, *Love in the Time of Cholera* would have done so. Although with reservations, the critic considers *Love in the Time of Cholera* superior to *One Hundred Years of Solitude* (239–244). *Love in the Time of Cholera* may be seen as the product of a more experienced author, who no longer needs the resources of magic realism and ambiguity to surprise the reader. There are other critics, by contrast, who find strong similarities between *Love in the Time of Cholera* and *One Hundred Years of Solitude*. Kathleen McNerney, for instance, finds that Florentino's letter writing can be thought of as constituting the novel itself, just as Melquíades' parchments tell the story of *One Hundred Years of Solitude* (McNerney 79). McNerney also points out the obvious about the novel by saying that the story is framed around an unusual love triangle (McNerney 74). The love triangle can be called unusual because one of the lovers is not physically involved but instead waits more than fifty years for his turn. It is also an unusual novel because the greatest lovers of all time have always been depicted as young, not old. With García Márquez's novel, readers around the world are reminded that love is ageless, in the sense that lovers do not have to be young to fall in love. Although falling in love may indeed be a common practice among the elderly, societal and cultural etiquette views such love as inappropriate and even shameful, as the character of Ofelia, Fermina's daughter, expresses it in the novel. However, neither the aging of Florentino and Fermina, society, nor anything else can interfere with the sublime love the old couple shares.

Love in the Time of Cholera, like all Gabriel García Márquez's works, explores the solitude of the individual and of humankind. In this novel, the existential anguish of feeling alone is portrayed through the solitude of love and of being in love.

PLOT DEVELOPMENT

Curiosity and suspense are two key words in understanding the plot of *Love in the Time of Cholera*. The reader feels the curiosity of a private detective in trying to figure out who Jeremiah Saint-Amour is, why he committed suicide, and what he wrote in the eleven-page letter he left for Dr. Juvenal Urbino. Who is Jeremiah's lover, and who is this man named Florentino Ariza? The latter shows up at the doctor's funeral and tells the widow: "I have waited for this opportunity for more than half a century, to repeat to you once again my vow of eternal fidelity and everlasting love" (64).

The novel's opening chapter foreshadows the importance of Dr. Juvenal Urbino and his wife, Fermina Daza, but most readers would not expect this since Dr. Urbino dies before the end of the first chapter. Naively, the reader may expect to see Dr. Juvenal Urbino bury his friend, Jeremiah Saint-Amour, at five in the afternoon. Instead, in disbelief, the reader learns that the doctor dies, after lunch on the same day, for the absurd reason of trying to catch a parrot. The narrator continually contradicts any suppositions readers may have made regarding the plot. This type of narrative stimulates readers to continue with the long, and at times slow-moving, love story.

The plot of *Love in the Time of Cholera* is, among other possibilities, about learning to wait, about perseverance and endurance, and about never forsaking the object of one's love. However, it is also about eternal fidelity and everlasting love, as Florentino Ariza stated it in the previous quotation.

Subsequent chapters take readers back in time to a story of love at first sight. If the novel followed a traditional linear plot line, it would have started with the second chapter, when Florentino, at age eighteen, meets Fermina, who is thirteen. The background of the plot is that of a port city, Cartagena de Indias, in the coastal northeast of Colombia, which has suffered through cholera panic and countless civil wars. The different social spheres of the plot's background depict an impoverished and dying wealthy class; an emerging middle class, which includes foreigners; and the poor classes, which make up two-thirds of the total population. The poor classes include mulattos and blacks, plus a few Chinese who account for a small Chinatown of four streets.

Nothing seems impossible for the young lovers, Florentino Ariza and Fermina Daza. While the two seem determined to fight for one another against all odds, Fermina's father, Lorenzo Daza, an illiterate Spanish immigrant, is equally decided to marry Fermina well. He strongly believes in upward mobility, and his last resort is his daughter's wedding. Florentino, being poor, is not a choice of whom Fermina's father will approve, but Fermina persists in her relationship with Florentino despite her father's wishes. However, after receiving four years of love letters, poems, telegrams, and music written and played just for her, Fermina suddenly tells Florentino that what she feels is not love. It is all an illusion, a spell she no longer believes in and wants no part of. Her reaction seems as unexpected and childlike as her reaction when they first met.

What readers thought was a perfect example of a fairy tale is thus ended by a stubborn young protagonist. Is Fermina indeed out of love or is her statement a reaction to her father telling her they are ruined? She turns her back on Florentino but he does not give up. Instead, he waits for the opportunity to reassure her of his love when they meet once again: fifty-one years, nine months, and four days later, at the funeral of Fermina's husband, Dr. Juvenal Urbino.

During those years, with Florentino Ariza out of the picture, Dr. Juvenal Urbino's persistence triumphs over the indifference of the young and beautiful Fermina. They first meet as doctor and patient (140). Dr. Juvenal Urbino goes to the wrong house, looking for an eighteen year-old girl who is supposed to be suffering from symptoms of cholera. Perhaps because he pays no attention to Fermina's flowering beauty, she thinks he is a selfish man, unable to love anyone other than himself. Fermina's father, however, is very taken with the doctor's family name. Eventually, the beautiful young girl, who is scorned and ridiculed by the social group to which Dr. Urbino belongs, goes on to marry the town's most eligible bachelor. Her wedding is splendid and unforgettable. The ultimate glory of the wedding is that the three-term president of the country attends (188). Does Dr. Juvenal Urbino love her? According to the omniscient narrator, Juvenal Urbino is aware that he does not love Fermina. Although he marries her out of physical attraction and even vanity, on their honeymoon he realizes that he could, indeed, fall in love with her.

Their Paris honeymoon lasts sixteen months, and the small-town girl learns of fashion, art, and literature. In this city, where Dr. Juvenal Urbino went to medical school, the young couple wants to see Victor Hugo, the French romantic writer, for whom Dr. Juvenal Urbino has a special liking, but they have to be content with the shared memory of glancing at Oscar Wilde (the Irish writer, poet, and dramatist who died in Paris). By the time the young married couple comes back to Cartagena de Indias, Fermina is six months pregnant with her first child.

After seeing Fermina coming out of church, pregnant with her first child, Florentino Ariza makes the decision "to win fame and fortune in order to deserve her" (199). He decides to wait "even till the end of time" (199). However, in a prejudiced society, economic success is not enough for a man whose bloodlines are unknown. Florentino Ariza was baptized, although he is a bastard, "a child of the street" in Spanish vernacular. He is the son of an unwed mother and a father who died without leaving him anything. Florentino's mother is herself an illegitimate child. Despite this background, Florentino Ariza manages to work his way up to become president of the River Company of the Caribbean—the only such company existing for the past one hundred years. During the entire time while Florentino waits to talk to Fermina again (fifty-one years, nine months, and four days), he never stops thinking about her, but he has many affairs, which he refers to as noncommitted love. He keeps a diary (actually, twenty-five in all), where he records the affairs of 622 lovers all grouped under one title: *They* (the feminine plural form in Spanish is *Ellas*). Some of these affairs appear as subplots interconnected to the main plot. These female lovers, each with their own strong will and sexuality, contribute to the strengthening of character that Fermina would observe later on, and even admire. Most of the lovers are widows. However, there are also married women; single women such as Leona Cassiani, with whom his affair lasts, off-and-on, for thirty years; prostitutes; and an incestuous affair with América Vicuña, a fourteen-year-old blood relative, who is entrusted to him by her own parents. Most readers, whether male or female, would question Florentino's conduct in light of his vow of eternal fidelity and everlasting love to Fermina. What kind of man could be so callous as to mislead a fourteen-year-old relative (who ends up committing suicide)? Is this something only a bastard, a son of the streets, would do?

Florentino feels inferior to Dr. Juvenal Urbino. They are members of two very different social classes, which is also true of Dr. Juvenal Urbino and Fermina Daza. However, the two classes converge into one for Juvenal and Fermina. This is not the case for Florentino and Fermina, despite Florentino's accomplishments and contributions to society.

Fermina becomes a faithful and loving wife. She fulfills her obligations both as wife and mother, and she grows to be the perfect consort for an important public figure. They have a son, Marco Aurelio, who becomes a doctor, thus continuing the family tradition; and a daughter, Ofelia, who is as beautiful as Fermina Daza was when she was young. Fermina's father, Lorenzo Daza, was a successful outlaw who was asked to leave his country because the governor of the province knew he had ignored all human and divine laws (254). When Lorenzo Daza dies, Fermina does not wear mourning but cries for him secretly. Fermina's strong character hardly ever breaks. Among the few times she does break is when her husband is adulterous. At age fifty-eight, the specter of infidelity enters the heart of Dr. Juvenal Urbino. He has an affair with Miss Bárbara Lynch, "a tall, elegant, large-boned mulatta" (292), who is a doctor of theology. Fermina's anger, interestingly enough, is not so much because of her husband's infidelity but because her honor is the subject of gossip and, also, because Bárbara Lynch is black. As a result of her husband's indiscretion, Fermina leaves the house for two years. She goes to live with her cousin Hildebranda in the countryside.

After reading about all these happenings, the reader is brought back again to the present time. It has been two weeks since the doctor died and two weeks since Florentino spoke to Fermina. It is at this point that the plot continues.

Fermina and Florentino's love story can be clearly seen in two parts. The first is when Florentino ingeniously, but unsuccessfully, tries to conquer Fermina's love. Although he is not experienced, he manages to win her attention and innocent teenage love until she comes to realize that she does not love him. The second part takes place at the end of their lives. She is now seventy-two years old and he is seventy-seven. He persists in his love for her, and Fermina, although still firm and strong of character, accepts him.

The abundance of literature that Florentino Ariza absorbed in his childhood and his extraordinary ability to write are two elements that contribute greatly to the novel's plot. Florentino wins Fermina over, both the first and the second times, with the letters he writes to her. The first time they are both teenagers. Their relationship, at that time, is exclusively based on Florentino's love letters, to which Fermina responds with equal passion. They hardly ever have a chance to talk, to interact, or to get to know each other. Their relationship during the first part, although strongly passionate, is rather precarious. The passion they both experience is such that Florentino proposes and she accepts. However, their childlike game has gone too far and the spell is broken for Fermina.

When they meet again nearly sixty years later, for most of which time Fermina was married, she rejects Florentino once more. It is at this time, nevertheless, that Florentino starts to write to Fermina again. His letters are formal in the beginning, in an effort to console her, but later he changes to a seductive mode. Florentino is not as graceful and handsome as Dr. Juvenal Urbino, but the power of his penmanship and his wholehearted insistence give him the edge that he needs to win her love. His tenacity—obsession, even—convinces Fermina that it is never too late to love. The novel ends on this upbeat note.

Although labyrinthine, the plot of *Love in the Time of Cholera* is rather accessible, even for first-time readers of Gabriel García Márquez. One can easily recognize the causality of events, even though they are not presented in strict chronological order—the novel begins in medias res (in the middle of things). The plot begins with the teenage love of Florentino and Fermina. The crux (the central or critical point) and longest part of *Love in the Time of Cholera* is what happens while Florentino and Fermina live separate lives. This time frame allows for personal growth and the maturation of the concept of love. The denouement coincides with the last chapter of the novel. Near the end, Fermina muses over how a person can be happy for so many years, through good times and bad, without even knowing if the emotion was really love (399). The novel culminates with the couple making love again and again. This is an elderly couple that is happy to be together and to be alive. Their relationship seemed hopeless except for Florentino's chronic romanticism and tireless desire to love Fermina. However, what unites this couple in love is the combination of Florentino's perseverance and Fermina's strong character. In the end, it is Fermina who faces the toughest battle in order to love. The battle that seems to summarize her will and determination is the one against her own daughter, Ofelia, who believes that love at her mother's age is revolting. Ofelia insists that Florentino's reputation, as everyone knows, is that of a pervert, and that Fermina's relationship with him will only do harm to the family's name. Fermina's response is a categorical, "they can all go to hell" (392).

GENRE AND NARRATIVE STRUCTURE

Love in the Time of Cholera is an intentional return to nineteenth-century realism and the outright fantasy we associate with García Márquez is absent, asserted critic Gene H. Bell-Villada (Bell-Villada 191). However, although there is plenty of realism in *Love in the Time of Cholera*, realism alone does not circumscribe the novel. Realism, in its purest form, rejects imaginative idealizations in favor of a detailed reality and sometimes focuses on triviality and the sordid aspects of life and nature. Realism is obvious in *Love in the Time of Cholera* in the portrayal of people's attitudes, physical settings, and material conditions. The descriptions of Florentino, Fermina, and Juvenal Urbino in the novel are so detailed and complete as to make them picture perfect, in the sense that the reader can almost see them as if in person; this technique is highly favored by realism. The same is true for the deplorable conditions in which the poor live, which is certainly emphasized in the decay of nature along the Magdalena River. The reality of the description discloses the exploitation of a dying nature. It is interesting to note the parallelism between the aging of Florentino and the decay of nature in the scenes where he takes the second trip down the Magdalena River, this time with Fermina. Furthermore, like a realist novel, *Love in the Time of Cholera* favors the lives of the middle and lower classes. The time frame of the novel, on the one hand, also calls for realism, for realism was most prominent in France between 1850 and 1880, around the time when Fermina and Juvenal Urbino lived in Paris for eighteen months. On the other hand, between 1880 and 1910 most Latin American writers began experimenting with realism as a literary form and the Latin American countries experienced social and cultural changes along with foreign investment. In Latin American literature this new reality adopted the French and Spanish tradition of realism, which tries to depict a faithful representation of life.

While this is indeed true for a realist novel, it is not necessarily the case for *Love in the Time of Cholera*. The detailed representation of both people and nature in *Love in the Time of Cholera* seems to come up short when it comes to the idealization of Fermina by Florentino. The concept of love itself loses its entire realist meaning and changes the novel into a *realist romantic* novel, which is a combination of the two. Unlike the objectivity of realism, the love of Florentino for Fermina is totally subjective. Like a true romantic, Florentino believes in the idea of dying for love. He dresses in black, the favorite color of romantics; he reads and writes poetry; and his face is pale like the descriptions of romantic poets. While love as a theme does not necessarily call for romanticism (love in literature can be traced as far back as the Middle Ages), *Love in the Time of Cholera* depicts love both realistically and romantically.

Unlike many of García Márquez's works, including his first book, *Leaf Storm*, *Love in the Time of Cholera* does not reflect an experimental structure. There is no shift in viewpoint and no use of stream of consciousness, two rather typical examples of experimental structure in García Márquez's writing. However, the structure at the start of *Love in the Time of Cholera* will not seem strange to readers of García Márquez. As is the case with most of his writing, *Love in the Time of Cholera* starts with a technique most commonly used in motion pictures: in medias res, or in the middle (see Chapter 3). At the very start of the novel the reader is presented with a dead man that the reader knows nothing about. The omniscient narrator provides any and all information. The death of Jeremiah Saint-Amour, a secondary character, provides the opportunity the narrator needs to talk about love between socially and economically displaced blacks, in the same way that the death of Dr. Juvenal Urbino provides the opportunity to talk about love among the ruling class. The death of Dr. Juvenal Urbino also takes place in the first chapter when he is eighty-one years old. The first chapter, which opens in medias res, sets up the story, which is told thereafter in chronological format, which is easier to read but not often used by García Márquez. The events are narrated in a linear fashion, following the lives of Fermina Daza and Florentino Ariza. (The narrative structure of the novel could have started with Chapter 2 had it been a completely linear narrative.)

An interesting way of viewing the structure of *Love in the Time of Cholera* is suggested by the epigraph that appears at the start of the novel, which suggests that the structure be viewed as a song, a *vallenato*. The epigraph reads:

> The words I am about to express:
> They now have their own crowned goddess.
> Leandro Díaz.

To Florentino, Fermina is indeed the *diosa coronada*, the crowned goddess. Florentino repeats the verse verbatim at least five times throughout the novel. The first time is when Florentino sees Fermina dressed in what looks like a Greek tunic, with a garland of fresh gardenias in her hair that "made her look like a crowned goddess" (74).

Where does this epigraph come from and who is Leandro Díaz? The epigraph itself is part of a *vallenato*, a musical genre that normally talks about folk heroes, love affairs, and other quarrels and was influenced by a combination of African, European, and folkloric Indian sounds. Leandro Díaz is among the best-known singer/songwriters of such genre. However, *vallenato* music is an obscure genre hardly known outside Colombia. Why then would García Márquez select such a little-known musician? The epigraphs in *Leaf Storm* (1955), *Chronicle of a Death Foretold* (1981), *The General in His Labyrinth* (1989), and *Of Love and Other Demons* (1994) bear the names of people who are highly recognizable. The epigraph in *Leaf Storm* is by Sophocles, one of classical Athens's three great playwrights (the other two being Aeschylus and Euripides). The epigraph in *Chronicle of a Death Foretold* is by Gil Vicente, a Portuguese dramatist of the sixteenth century who wrote both in Spanish and Portuguese. *The General in His Labyrinth* contains an epigraph by Simón Bolívar, the South American liberator. In *Of Love and Other Demons* the epigraph is by Thomas Aquinas, the Italian religious philosopher of the Middle Ages turned saint who, to date, is still one of the most influential theologians of the Catholic Church.

García Márquez's choice of a relative unknown, Leandro Díaz, is consistent with his tendency to favor popular culture, which he views as the source of all culture, and it also signals the autobiographical nature of the story, which mirrors the love relationship between his own parents (see Chapter 1).

Another point regarding García Márquez's selection of this musician relates to the manner in which he sometimes thinks of his writings. The Colombian magazine *Cambio* (*Change*) quoted him as saying that *One Hundred Years of Solitude* is a 400-page *vallenato* and *Love in the Time of Cholera*, a 380-page *bolero*. *Bolero* is another form of Latin American music, whose dance is also known as *bolero*. While the *vallenato* talks about single folk heroes, such as Colonel Aureliano Buendía in *One Hundred Years of Solitude*, *boleros* normally depict love songs where the lovers go through penance, suffering, and often rejection, as in *Love in The Time of Cholera*.

CHARACTER DEVELOPMENT

Character development in *Love in the Time of Cholera* depends both on the consciousness of the omniscient narrator and on the consciousness of the characters as they interact in the novel's story line. *Love in the Time of Cholera* presents fewer characters than *One Hundred Years of Solitude*. The illusion in the former, however, is the same as in the latter. A reader envisions tumultuous crowds, large gatherings, parties, celebrations, and crowded neighborhoods with lots of people on the streets. They see a moviehouse with no empty seats, vibrant cities and towns, and people everywhere: at church, traveling, walking down the streets of Cartagena de Indias, the Colombian country side, and the streets of Paris. Most of the people in these crowds are only references without names. Some of them exist in the memory of the reader for what they were doing at the moment of the narrative, as if in a snapshot. The president of the republic is merely an enunciation, as is Dr. Adrien Proust, the father of the famous French writer Marcel Proust, and the twenty-eighth president of the United States, Woodrow Wilson. It is the same with other established literary figures, fashion designers, and generals who participated in the Colombian civil wars. They come in and out of the narrative as a sketch. Although this is true for most of the minor characters, the main characters are carefully and meticulously drawn.

Fermina Daza, Juvenal Urbino, and Florentino Ariza are developed from a social and psychological viewpoint. These viewpoints are strongly enriched by the moral and religious principles that the characters share. Whereas Fermina and Florentino appear as the two pillars on which the novel stands, Juvenal Urbino is strong enough to shake the structure and change the course of the narrative. Through the plot, which is seemingly simple yet abundant in detailed information, the reader gains extensive knowledge of who Fermina, Juvenal, and Florentino really are. The reader may end up judging them, but the author does not; without judgment, the narrative includes their likes and dislikes, preferences, shortcomings, reactions, and ambitions.

Fermina's character is developed in three clearly defined phases. These three phases are marked by significant details within the novel. The first phase can be observed when she is a teenage girl living in her father's house. At that time Fermina is described as long-boned, slim, with steel-blue hair and clear almond eyes, and an inborn haughtiness, diligent, and of strong character (41). She loves flowers, birds, and domestic animals. Fermina's haughtiness, stubbornness, and cleverness can be seen when her father sends her away, on a journey to forget (102). However, the plan does not work, as the two young lovers find a way to communicate by telegraph. When Fermina returns, a year and half later, her father thinks that his daughter has forgotten her young lover. However, when she opens the balcony window the morning after their arrival, "she no longer thought of him as the impossible sweetheart but as the certain husband to whom she belonged heart and soul" (121). Most readers are therefore astonished when she decides to end the relationship, which she now sees as a chimera. With her first sight of Florentino after their long separation, the spell is broken. She argues that their love is just an illusion (126). The reader may think that her reaction is immature (recall that she is only seventeen), but the author does not comment.

The second phase in Fermina's character development starts with the realization of her father's dream "to turn his daughter into a great lady" (100). Lorenzo Daza wants a propitious marriage for his daughter Fermina, which results in a marriage of convenience to the renowned doctor Juvenal Urbino. Throughout her marriage, she adapts to an upper social class but never fully embraces it. She turns into a serious, faithful, and responsible woman. Hers is a stable, perfect family: a hard-working husband and two children, a boy and a girl. Of the three phases of her life, this is the longest and most tedious.

The third phase in Fermina's character development comes when she reencounters Florentino at the death of her husband, after fifty-one years, nine months, and four days. Fermina behaves as a respectable widow, mature and self-controlled, but Florentino eventually manages to win her over. She then gives herself totally, generously sharing with him a kind of love perhaps neither had ever experienced before.

Dr. Juvenal Urbino de la Calle is meticulously developed. As readers we become aware of the smallest details of his personality and of his roles as doctor, professor, socialite, and even lover, both faithful and unfaithful. He is the personification of correctness. In all aspects of his life he seems perfect: socially, aesthetically, economically, religiously, and (almost) morally. He is the scion of a distinguished family. He completed advanced studies in medicine and surgery in Paris. He is knowledgeable in his field, in literature, in music, and in fashion; he is captivating and seducing; he is a good dancer and pianist; he possesses all the graces to make him, at the age of twenty-eight, "the most desirable of bachelors" (128). He favors classical music and prefers French literature to Spanish authors. For this purpose, he has a bookseller who periodically sends him the latest publications from Paris. Among other authors, he reads Anatole France, Pierre Loti, Remy de Gourmont, Paul Bourget, Oscar Wilde, and Victor Hugo (195–97). Although he is a practicing and extremely pious Catholic, who invokes the Holy Spirit and punctually attends all religious functions, he is unfaithful to his wife. He betrays her with Bárbara Lynch, a beautiful mulatta with whom he enjoys the pleasures of a passionate affair (291–304). Consistent with his religious and moral principles, however, he repents. He confesses to his wife, asks her to forgive him, and remains faithful until he dies. However, behind all this correctness, his real self is somehow camouflaged. Indeed, he is conscious that he is not in love with his wife. He loves her exterior, but they are not compatible in temperament.

Florentino Ariza, in very many ways, is the antithesis of Dr. Juvenal Urbino. He is everything Juvenal Urbino is not. He is homely and sickly looking, has no sense of fashion, comes from a poor and broken family, holds no university degrees (in fact, he may not have finished high school), is not a practicing Catholic, prefers to read minor Spanish authors, is not a socialite, and seems to have no direction in life. However, of all the characters, he is the one who feels love the most; he loves passionately and with tremendous abandonment.

As with Fermina, Florentino's character can be seen in three stages of development. The first stage presents Florentino as a phantom-like character. He lives a quiet life, passing unnoticed in the crowd. His only reason for existence is to watch Fermina walk through the park on her way to school and back. Other than the time he spends as a clerk at the post office, he passes most of his time reading and writing love letters to Fermina.

This platonic love, which is more spiritual than physical, ends after three years with a vitrious rejection by Fermina. However, the flame of his passion for her does not fade. He waits—for fifty-one years, nine months, and four days—to reiterate his love for her.

The second developmental stage, which covers the near half-century between their meetings, turns Florentino into a man of business and of great social and economic success. His phantom-like appearance is now only the disguise for a life of indiscriminate sex. He had wanted to keep himself a virgin, to honor Fermina, but fails. From writing letters to Fermina in the first stage, he turns to writing a diary of his love affairs, and in twenty-five booklets he records 622 entries. Despite these many affairs, however, he remains single, hoping one day to marry Fermina. However, he may never have imagined how long he would have to wait.

The third stage finds Florentino an old man, bald and wearing dentures. His love for Fermina has not changed, but neither has her stubbornness, for she rejects him again at her husband's funeral. This time, however, the rejection lasts only two weeks. Over the course of the following year, in the same way he did when they were young, Florentino writes Fermina 132 letters, and this time he wins her love. Florentino Ariza is given a second chance, and this time he is ready. He has undergone a complete metamorphosis, including his dress code (the only thing he would not change before). Florentino, from the start, is a kind of Eros (the god of love in Greek mythology), and it is his character that sustains the narrative.

It is interesting to see how García Márquez plays with the symbolism of names, as if he wanted to challenge the reader's response regarding the moral values of Florentino. Florentino Ariza is a son of the streets, a bastard, by the mere fact that his father would not recognize him; *son of the streets* in Spanish is *hijo de la calle*. This is very close to the name that Dr. Juvenal Urbino holds proudly as part of his noble name: The doctor's full name is Juvenal Urbino de la Calle, with a capital *C*.

There are also many secondary characters whose presences contribute to the changes the main characters go through. Aunt Escolástica is a loving, illiterate spinster who raises Fermina as if she were her own until the day her brother realizes that she is responsible for letting Florentino come close to his daughter. Then he sends her, penniless, back to San Juan de la Ciénaga.

Lorenzo Daza, Fermina's father, is an upstart who leaves Spain looking for a better future. In the Colombian mountain region, in San Juan de la Ciénaga, the illiterate Spaniard's good fortune begins when he marries Fermina Sánchez, a rich farm girl whose parents are against her love for Lorenzo Daza. Lorenzo Daza's wife gives birth to a girl called Fermina, like her mother. After his wife's death, Lorenzo, his daughter, and his sister,

Escolástica, move to the coastal city of Cartagena de Indias. Although lacking social skills, Lorenzo Daza buys and remodels an old colonial house in the Park of the Evangelists. A strong disciplinarian, he rules his house with an iron fist. He lacks the company of friends, enjoys drinking, and gets involved in illegal business.

Among the long list of 622 lovers are several worth mentioning, including Leona Cassiani, Sara Noriega, Olimpia Zuleta, Prudencia Pitre, Angeles Alfaro, and Ausencia Santander. Leona Cassiani represents, by far, the longest of the 622 affairs. (In the section on a feminist reading of this chapter, the reader can find more information regarding this character.) Sara Noriega, who is overweight but happy, can be best described as a "Fat Venus." She is particularly important as a lover because she is Florentino's projection as a poet. He stays with her for several years, and records in his diary that he loved her. She is forty years old, ten years older than Florentino, yet she cannot climax unless she sucks on an infant's pacifier (238). Olimpia Zuleta is among the shortest-lived affairs. She is a married woman whom it took Florentino six months to seduce. Olimpia finally gives in to desire and goes to bed with him, on a beautiful afternoon in one of his riverboats. However, an obscenity written by Florentino on her belly causes the story to end in tragedy. That same night, when Olimpia goes to bed, "having forgotten what was scrawled there," she undresses in front of her husband, who, with a single slash of his razor, cuts her throat (263).

Prudencia Pitre is a widow like many of the women whom Florentino recorded in his diary. However, Prudencia Pitre is known as the Widow of Two because she has outlived two husbands. Like all his lovers, Angeles Alfaro, a music teacher whom Florentino describes in his diary as "the ephemeral one," teaches Florentino something about love. He records that with her (although he had already experienced this before), "one can be in love with several people at the same time, feel the same sorrow with each, and not betray any of them" (328). Ausencia Santander, like many of the female characters in *Love in the Time of Cholera*, displays a total independence regarding her sexuality. It is unclear, says the narrator, whether her husband left her or she left him. Hers was a conventional marriage. They had three children, the children got married, and she began to see men at her own desire. Besides teaching him about love, all his lovers, argues Florentino Ariza, contributed to his need for being loved, for understanding love itself.

Florentino's long list of lovers seems to contribute more to *Love in the Time of Cholera* than the character development of Fermina's son and daughter; Marco Aurelio Urbino Daza and Ofelia Urbino Daza.

THEMATIC ISSUES

It may seem obvious that love is the central theme in *Love in the Time of Cholera*. However, the theme of love in this novel is multifaceted; it can be looked at from different perspectives. Among other thematic possibilities are the evils of a socially divided city and the implicit acts of reading and writing. All these themes, however, are intertwined and, as a result, it is difficult to separate one from the other. The theme of love, however, is the only one that encompasses them all, and it is therefore examined in the most detail.

The impetuous, idealistic, strong, and youthful love between Florentino and Fermina is totally platonic. It starts with a look, which soon turns into a gaze. Theirs is certainly the "look of love." Florentino, at that time an apprentice at the Postal Agency, takes a telegram to Lorenzo Daza's home address and sees the young girl reading. Fermina raises her eyes to see who is coming "and that casual glance was the beginning of a cataclysm of love that had not ended half a century later" (68). Florentino's love is awakened first. When it starts, he is content to sit in the park by her house, to see her walk by four times a day, always in the company of her aunt, Escolástica. As Florentino feels his love grow stronger, he moves from the passive mode of seeing to a more active mode, that of writing. To declare his love to her, he writes a sixty-page letter using both sides of each page. Thus starts an epistolary love affair of immeasurable frequency and intensity. It is precisely the letter writing, and not the physical encounters, that makes their love possible. In fact, over a three-year period they only have the opportunity to talk three times. The first time is an afternoon at the end of January when Florentino wants to give Fermina a letter but she rejects it, arguing that she does not have her father's permission. The second time is a week later, when she accepts the letter and they exchange only a few words. The third time is to receive an answer to his letter; since she has none, he insists, saying that it is a lack of courtesy to accept a letter and not to answer it. That is the last time they talk for over fifty years. Their epistolary is all they have and is what causes her expulsion from her school. Fermina's father tries to convince her that love at her age is an illusion; he wants her to beg for forgiveness to get back into the Academy and offers her help finding happiness with a worthy suitor (99). However, Fermina, as her name implies, remains firm in her love for Florentino and does not give up. In despair, after talking with Florentino, who has also decided not to give up, Lorenzo Daza decides to take his daughter away to make her forget. They go back to the small town where they came from, San Juan de la Ciénaga. Paradoxically, although their postal contact does not stop while she is away, a love that seemed eternal crumbles when she, once again, sees him. After coming back from her trip, Fermina writes Florentino a two-line letter asking him to please "forget it" (126).

Another facet of love, no less interesting than the first, is that of love between the married couple, Fermina Daza and Dr. Juvenal Urbino. Although the omniscient narrator suggests that Fermina married for convenience, there are ample suggestions that this sentiment changes over time. She enjoys her wedding trip, lovemaking, and living in Paris. After sixteen months, upon returning to Cartagena de Indias pregnant with her first child, she feels like "the happiest woman on earth" (194).

After some years, the couple goes back to Europe to renew a love that was beginning to decay because of the drudgeries and sameness of the daily routine. As a result of this second honeymoon, Fermina comes back pregnant once again. The instances of love that she shows for her husband are many, particularly the gestures of love in their old age. In the last few minutes before his death, the omniscient narrator discloses that between them there was indeed a true love, a love that Dr. Juvenal Urbino seemed to realize he had failed to communicate to her, when he speaks his last words, "only God knows how much I loved you" (56). Dr. Urbino is more a spiritual man than a physical one. He loves Fermina conceptually, for being his wife and the mother of his children, rather than for being the woman she is. He is rather incapable of looking at sex without pondering the scientific insight regarding how the human body functions. His moral and religious values do not allow him to be a good lover, at home or elsewhere. With the sensuous and sexual, young, beautiful Miss Lynch, the sex act becomes comical but sad. He spends the exact amount of time needed to give an injection during a routine visit (298). However, for Fermina, being conceptually happy is not enough. After returning from the honeymoon happy and remaining so for six years (until they move to their own house), she feels like a prisoner in a strange house and, even worse, that she is with a man who was not her dream (249). During that time, Fermina comes to believe that behind the professional authority and worldly charm of her husband there is a hopeless weakling (250). When they move into their own house, things are not much different. While she is loved, catered to, and even feared in public, at home she feels like a deluxe servant, not a loved wife (268). While discussing this second facet of love— the love between Fermina and Dr. Urbino—it is worth noting what Fermina feels for Florentino. Although she represses any feeling toward him, the narrator reveals that she often thinks of him. During the fifty-one years while she is married to Juvenal Urbino, she thinks of Florentino with compassion and nostalgia; she even feels tormented by guilt (247).

The third facet of love is described in the last chapter of the novel. Fermina is now seventy-two years old and Florentino is seventy-seven. He feels he has the right to make up for lost time and on the very day of her husband's burial, he expresses once again his vow of everlasting love, but again she rejects him.

Although Florentino and Fermina are now an elderly couple, their ability to deal with love seems unchanged. Once again, the means of bringing them together is letter writing, which is how they express their feelings. This time it is Fermina who writes first, sending a three-page letter full of insults. Over the following year, Florentino writes her 132 letters. He starts writing once a week, then twice a week, and then every day. While Fermina does not answer any of the letters, she keeps them to find solace and to reflect upon Florentino's writing. On the first anniversary of her husband's death, Florentino attends the memorial mass, without being invited. This is his chance to talk to Fermina again. She greets him and thanks him for coming.

Two weeks later Florentino comes to visit her. Although he is uninvited and unannounced, she receives him, nevertheless. Hereafter, their Tuesday visits are as frequent and consoling as the letters, and they become great friends. Fermina's son approves of their relationship, but her daughter does not. Ofelia tenaciously opposes, arguing that love at their age "is revolting" (392). Neither Ofelia, the rumor of Florentino's homosexuality, nor anything else convinces Fermina to stop seeing him. Instead, she accepts Florentino's invitation to go on a riverboat cruise along the Magdalena River. Playfully, García Márquez gives the boat the name *New Fidelity*. The couple's unstoppable drive to be together is finally realized.

A different facet of love that the novel brings to the reader's attention is unfaithfulness. Violating the marriage vows, Dr. Juvenal Urbino embarks on an extramarital affair. Contrary to his impeccable correctness at home, in public, and in his profession, Dr. Urbino breaks social and racial codes and, after thirty years of marriage, falls in love with Bárbara Lynch. Thirty years younger, the beautiful twenty-eight-year old mulatta causes the marriage to crumble. Dr. Urbino's desire for Bárbara Lynch is out of control. He thinks of her all day and, incapable of stopping his passion, he feels the torment of guilt. After six months he ends the affair, but Fermina leaves him and stays away for two years.

Florentino Ariza enjoys yet another kind of love, if, indeed, promiscuous affairs with over 600 women can be described as a form of love. As a kind of hunter, Florentino engages in casual love. Florentino responds to raw desire. His sex partners are simply outlets to appease his desire and ward off his desperate solitude. Regardless, however, he feels they all teach him something.

The second theme in *Love in the Time of Cholera* is the division of classes in society. The difference between rich and poor in the novel is remarkable. Although the novel does not suggest the existence of any turmoil or open conflict between the different social classes, the disparities are obvious to the reader. The social, economic, and racial scenery of the novel brings to the forefront a small group of rich, white people, among which the Urbino de la Calle family is one of the most prestigious. This group constitutes the ruling class: it includes civil authorities, the high ranks of the military, and a few impoverished aristocratic families. Different racial groups make up the balance of the classes and represent the majority: Chinese immigrants, blacks, mulattos, and Indians, many of whom live in abject poverty. A good number of these people work as slave-like servants in the households of the wealthy.

The novel repeatedly takes notice of the differences between the rich and the poor. While the rich live in the ancestral homes in the district of the Viceroys and the residential district of La Manga, the aspiring middle classes live elsewhere. The poor live in a section of the city where the landscape includes pestilence, unnumbered houses, loud music, and children running around nude—a part of the city not surprisingly known as the old slave quarter—which is a death trap for the poor (23).

The rich in the novel attend lavish parties. They accompany their celebrations and dances with string quartets, bands, and orchestras playing music by Mozart and Schubert. Although the poor are seen everywhere, the rich do not mingle with them. Upward mobility can be achieved through economic success, but entrance to social clubs of the elite is reserved for legitimate descendants, born into families with an ancestral name. The marked stratification of class is observed everywhere. At the cathedral, for example, the first few pews are reserved for their lifetime owners, whose names are engraved on copper nameplates on the back of the seats (360). The rest of the congregation can sit elsewhere; however, the poorest, being mostly mulattos and blacks, must sit in the back.

The novel also suggests that the boundary between rich and poor is not insurmountable. It is interesting to note that Lorenzo Daza, although a plebeian by birth, changes his fortune in life, as well as that of his daughter. Fermina, who because of her manners seems to define a new type of societal class, is the product of a well-thought-out, well-executed plan. First, Lorenzo Daza moves from the countryside to the coastal city to provide his daughter Fermina with the formal instruction she would need. He registers her in a religious school for rich girls. Then he manages to marry her to Dr. Juvenal Urbino. With this marriage, Fermina enters a social and economic world totally different from her own—a world she is not prepared to move into. Upon her return from her honeymoon and for six consecutive, painful, and hateful years, Fermina undergoes the "training" that her mother-in-law puts her through. While she learns and adapts to her new social class, she never fully abandons her roots, and she maintains her spontaneity, her love for nature, and a touch of crudeness in her speech.

Florentino Ariza is another example of someone who successfully changes his lot in life. Unlike Fermina's change of fate, his is the result of a decision of his own, made, not for upward mobility, but to make him worthy of Fermina's love. For thirty years, he works at all types of jobs within the River Company of the Caribbean, ending up as president of the Board of Directors, general manager, and, eventually, owner. He restores his house to reflect his new social economic status but also to be prepared to be worthy of Fermina Daza when his next opportunity comes along.

Another salient aspect on the theme of class division is the incorporation of mulattoes into different subplots within the novel. Jeremiah Saint-Love, the mulatto who kills himself at the outset of *Love in the Time of Cholera*, is Dr. Juvenal Urbino's friend. Two mulattas presented in the novel are alternately treated both as object and subject. Bárbara Lynch, some may argue, is the object of an elderly, powerful man who wants her for sexual favors. However, Dr. Urbino also expresses love for her. Leona Cassiani, also a mulatta, goes to all public functions with Florentino Ariza. She gains the respect of those with whom she works at the River Company of the Caribbean and moves into the highest ranks of the company. Florentino falls in love with her but she rejects him. In spite of this, however, they remain good friends.

An interesting aspect of the theme of a socially divided society is that it appears to be deteriorating. Fermina Daza, Florentino Ariza, and Leona Cassiani seem to signal a change in the social order, and to offer the availability of upward mobility. The old, rich, aristocratic, and insulated world of the elite, the highest social level (represented by families like the Urbinos de la Calle), is disappearing. Although the instances are many, the reader notices that the actions of Dr. Juvenal Urbino de la Calle seem to make the loudest statement of this change. First, he marries a woman outside his social class. Second, he moves from his former palace of the Marquis de Casalduero to a new house in a neighborhood of the *nouveaux riches* (the new rich). Third, and probably most significant, his family name will no doubt die with his children. His children, says the narrator, were two undistinguished ends of a line. His son, Marco Aurelio, continues the narrative, has done nothing worthy of note—he has not even produced a child. His daughter, Ofelia, has three daughters but no sons. Thus, the name, the tradition, and the old social order symbolically die with Dr. Urbino's children.

SOCIAL AND HISTORICAL CONTEXT

The reader may have the feeling that this is just a strange love story, but it is far more: the civil unrest, superstition, civil wars, disappearance of a colonial power, and birth of a new middle class that surround the love story are of significance in themselves. García Márquez goes to considerable efforts to document the historical setting of this novel. He uses actual historical figures such as the president of Colombia at the time of the tale, Rafael Núñez, a statesman and writer born in Cartagena de Indias (a favored physical setting of García Márquez's work), and several liberal generals in the Colombian armed forces, including Ricardo Gaitán Obeso, who, in fact, fought against the government of President Rafael Núñez. President Rafael Núñez and General Gaitán Obeso represent the two great opposing political forces in Colombia's government and in García Márquez's writing. The president was a member of the Conservative Party and the general was in the Liberal Party. The setting of *Love in the Time of Cholera* also includes, although as mere references, actual historical events such as the War of a Thousand Days and the massacre of striking banana workers in 1928.

Love in the Time of Cholera, on a much smaller scale than *One Hundred Years of Solitude*, is concerned with the Colombian civil wars of the last part of the nineteenth century and the violence of the first two decades of the twentieth century. These historical and political concerns, however, may pass unnoticed by the reader because that indeed is the intent. If *One Hundred Years of Solitude* disguises these concerns through the uses of myth, fantasy, hyperbole, and magic realism, *Love in the Time of Cholera* disguises them through its depiction of a long, sometimes exasperating, love affair. However, the cholera that appears like a sign in the title of the novel is, in fact, a bad omen and can be seen as a symbol of the historical violence that Colombia continues to undergo.

The superabundance of information in *Love in the Time of Cholera* will go unnoticed unless the reader is inquisitive and meticulous. For example, when García Márquez describes Fermina's bird, he says that it was bought right before the last civil war based on a rumor of an upcoming visit by the Pope. The government spread the rumor to scare the liberals. The reader, on the one hand, has to understand that the concept of a civil war is used to describe the ongoing political wars of liberals against conservatives that lasted through the 1960s; and, on the other hand, that the papal visit is indeed fictional, for no Pope ever visited Colombia until 1973. If the reader pays attention to references like this, then the novel can be seen to denounce what the government wanted to hide: the killings of people who appeared floating in the Magdalena River. There are allusions of discontent against the conservative government throughout the novel. Even the parrot, the indirect cause of Dr. Juvenal Urbino's death, shouts, "long live the Liberal Party damn it, a reckless cry that had cost many a carefree drunk his life" (33).

The time frame of the narrative pays close attention to a bygone era, some readers may say, and pays no attention to the violence that Colombia was undergoing in the mid-1980s, when *Love in the Time of Cholera* was published. There are readers, though, who may see the many references to violence, political turmoil, corruption, and the devastation of nature, along with the cholera in the title, as a way of pointing out that violence is a constant element of both social and political life in Colombia. If *Love in the Time of Cholera* were to be seen as irresponsible for not dealing with the oppression, violence, and the social and economic disparities that García Márquez is known to denounce, then the reader would still have to consider the treatment that García Márquez gives to love in this novel. Love in the novel is not carefree, easy flowing, spontaneous, and idealized. Although Florentino idealizes Fermina and the love he feels for her, everything around him is hostile. The narrative does not make life easy for an illegitimate child, Florentino, just because he is in love. As literary critic José Luis Méndez wrote, the social conventions, the economic ambitions, the ideological and political prejudices, and even the twisted understanding of patriotism, interfere with everyday life and the way the characters love and make love (Méndez 196). While it is true that love triumphs in the novel, García Márquez is not providing a model where love escapes social and biological laws, but rather the opposite. *Love in the Time of Cholera* refuses to accept the conventional time frame for falling in love and ignores the limitations thought to be imposed by aging; it rejects the fact that prestige and social rank must, in the end, destroy love, but furnishes the narration with the social and economic components that interfere with the love between Florentino and Fermina and between Dr. Juvenal Urbino and Fermina. Florentino has to undergo the transitional changes both socially and economically that make him deserving of Fermina's love, and Fermina has to learn the manners of the social group that she marries into when she marries Dr. Juvenal Urbino.

The comparison between *One Hundred Years of Solitude* and *Love in the Time of Cholera* mentioned in this chapter and observed by many readers and critics is perhaps inevitable. Almost everything García Márquez has written since the publication of *One Hundred Years of Solitude* in 1967 is compared to it. One of the best comparisons is that of sociologist and literary critic José Luis Méndez who points out that in *One Hundred Years of Solitude* there is no hope for starting anew, but in *Love in the Time of Cholera* there is hope for salvation through the power of love. The universe described by the narrative voice in *One Hundred Years of Solitude* is, in the end, completely destroyed "because races condemned to one hundred years of solitude did not have a second chance on earth," as the narrator explains in the closing paragraph of the novel (448). In *Love in the Time of Cholera*, however, in the end, the characters that inhabit the novel do not perish. The novel does not end with the total destruction of the universe it has created. A second chance on earth, which was denied to the characters of *One Hundred Years of Solitude*, is given to those who love in *Love in the Time of Cholera*.

Love is seen as the redeeming force that saves both humanity and its history. Love, then, appears as a driving force that defies everything. As if in biblical terms, the narrator seems to state that it is not yet too late to stop the end of humanity and to reach out for justice and happiness. However, there is no naive idealism in the narrative voice of the novel. Nothing is taken for granted, and the narrator is ready to remind us that the world around the characters of *Love in the Time of Cholera* is too oppressive to ignore. That is why the riverboat in which Fermina and Florentino travel, although utopian in its intent, sports a flag signaling cholera and cannot find a secure port to dock. The novel ends with the reader wondering if Fermina and Florentino will ever be able to come ashore and exercise their second chance.

Love, to García Márquez, is a kind of philosophical tool, a way of looking at the world. As the sociologist and literary critic José Luis Méndez pointed out, García Márquez expressed this philosophy "on love" three years before the publication of *Love in the Time of Cholera* when he addressed the Nobel Academy in Stockholm. On the occasion of accepting the Nobel Prize, García Márquez delivered a speech that argued against the scientific possibility of a nuclear disaster. In closing, Gabriel García Márquez spoke of a new utopia:

> Where no one will be able to decide for others how they die, where love will prove true and happiness possible, and where the races condemned to one hundred years of solitude will have, at last and forever, a second opportunity on earth. (García Márquez 1988, 91)

If the reader fails to see the political turmoil behind the story it is understandable, for once again, as in all of Gabriel García Márquez's writings, *Love in the Time of Cholera* is multilayered and can be read from multiple perspectives, depending on the reader. The art of storytelling is in the foreground, and this time readers of García Márquez will come away feeling they understand the book: it is a love story where reality is all around. It is a novel that is both romantic and realist.

ALTERNATIVE READING: FEMINIST THEORY

When a reader first hears the term *feminist*, he or she may immediately think in terms of the status of women. Feminism can be studied from different viewpoints: linguistic, political, economic, sociological, psychological, biological, or other. For some critics from developed nations of the Western world, it is nearly canonical that feminist literary criticism began with the women's movement that followed World War II. For such critics, the two most commonly referenced authors are Simone de Beauvoir and Kate Millett. However, dating the origin of feminism to these two authors seems rather simplistic if the reader realizes that the two books selected by such critics were not published until 1949, for *Le Deuxième Sexe* (*The Second Sex*) by Beauvoir; and 1970, for *Sexual Politics* by Millett. In *The Second Sex*, Beauvoir examines how male authors have developed female characters in literary texts.

The fight for equal rights for women, in whatever manner, however, goes back much further than 1949. By the turn of the twentieth century there was already a movement for women's suffrage (the right to vote). In fact, the struggle for women's rights may have started as early as the eighteenth century. Indeed, Mary Wollstonecraft published *A Vindication of the Rights of Woman* in 1792.

Nowadays, and as early as the late 1960s, those interested in feminist theory approached it as a subject of study in colleges and universities around the world. In a general way, feminist theory aims to accomplish the following:

- To review, expose, and critique those standards where the orientation is patriarchal, whether in literature, politics, civil rights, power, sexuality, race, and other aspects of life;
- To recover texts written by women that have been either forgotten, lost, or neglected;
- To understand the cultural parameters involved in the construction of gender and identity.

Many feminist critics, to some degree, continue to be misunderstood in the belief that the issues investigated by feminist theory not only have to be women centered, but also have to be seen from a woman's point of view. This not only excludes women who may look at a text from a viewpoint that disregards gender issues, but also prevents men from doing a feminist reading of any given text.

From a pedagogical point of view, feminist theory can be accepted as a method or technique to study a text. As such, the critic questions long-standing, dominant, male ideologies and patriarchal attitudes and interpretations of literature. Is such an approach more or less feminist because a male rather than a female critic carries it out? There is debate among feminists themselves on this question. According to American feminist writer and celebrity of the women's movement in the early and mid-1990s, Naomi Wolf, feminism "should be broadly understood as a humanistic movement for social justice" (139). Feminists in Latin America, possibly to gain support, sponsor the values of maternity and wifehood. They believe that these two roles bring reforms, first within the family, and thereafter within society as a whole. In literature, the Mexican writer Sara Sefchovich observes this in her novel *La señora de los sueños* (1993).

A feminist reading of *Love in the Time of Cholera* would show how the female characters are portrayed in the space and time where they live in the novel. Clearly, not all the female characters in the novel are alike, nor are the central female characters treated alike. A feminist reading might consider whether they reacted and responded in a manner often described as feminine (not feminist), regardless of social class, race, and education. The rich and educated women of the novel are not necessarily the ones with the strongest character or the women whom the male characters desire sexually, but they do exercise their own sexuality. The female characters in *Love in the Time of Cholera* are in control of their sexuality. They are developed as free, strong, and independent. They do not correspond to a stereotype, a ready-made model repeated by both male and female writers, where Latin American women are voiceless and submissive.

While *Love in the Time of Cholera* depicts such disparate female roles as those of mother and prostitute, neither one of the two characterizations lacks voice or will. The world of the novel is a matriarchal one. Without his mother, Fermina Daza, and all the women that come in and out of Florentino's life, the novel could not develop in the manner it does. Florentino Ariza and Juvenal Urbino are not sexist; they do not see women as inferior beings. Although, in itself, this is not a novel that shows the battle of the sexes, the roles played by women are the strongest. Even though written by a male, the novel points out significant signs of a matriarchal universe. To this extent, Gabriel García Márquez has expressed, in an interview with Ana Cristina Navarro, that women are the strong being, and thanks to them history is able to continue its normal course. My women, says the Colombian author, are more in touch with reality. They have their feet firmly planted on the ground. They are solid, patient, true. And García Márquez adds, men are creatures of dreams, capable of the most crazy and magnificent actions, but unable to be patient or trustworthy. They are weaklings in the face of adversity. They search for support in women, who are as firm as rocks. This, he concludes, is how the world is in Macondo and elsewhere.

Fermina Daza is certainly Florentino's sweetheart, and at the time of their youth, around the mid-1800s, she believes in romance and the power of the written word. To Fermina Daza, Florentino's letters carry more meaning than her own studies, her father, or even the Church. Her world, at the age of seventeen, is interrupted by her interfering father but never completely dominated by him. García Márquez provides her with a voice of her own. It is hard to imagine a young woman of the nineteenth century more independent than Fermina Daza. It is she who ends the relationship between herself and Florentino. She was fully aware when it started, and she calls it off without a tear or a fight, remaining in complete control. To neither of the two loves of her life—Florentino Ariza or Juvenal Urbino—is she an object. At all times she projects herself as a subject. She is a woman who is aware of her roles as mother, wife, friend, and public person. Fermina is stable, strong, confident, and poised. She knows exactly where she has been and where the winds of life are taking her. She fights for what she wants, and against a social world she does not embrace, old and decaying traditions of the noble families, hypocrisy and gossip, Ofelia, her own daughter (to defend Florentino), and her right to love and be loved.

Whereas the strength of Fermina is observed throughout the length of the book, the novel opens with the weakness of a male character who kills himself because he cannot endure the prospect of getting old. Jeremiah Saint-Amour, a photographer of children, commits suicide because he is turning sixty years old. Saint-Amour (the name translates into English as *Saint of Love*) is, without a doubt, the opposite of Fermina.

Love in the Time of Cholera contorts the roles of male and female characters that we are used to observing, but it does so without being biased or judgmental. Whereas the reader makes the association of a "Saint of Love" with Jeremiah's last name, García Márquez describes the black Haitian character as a saint but, he adds ironically, "An atheistic saint" (10). Another instance of contorting roles comes with the violence and sexual abuse inflicted on women during rape. Feminism looks at rape as a form of cultural oppression. In rape, women are treated as sex objects. The psychological scars of rape are so deep that most women have difficulty ever seeing themselves as subjects of love again. In *Love in the Time of Cholera*, this situation is inverted. The sexual assault is on a man, Florentino Ariza, whose rape is the result of a plan elaborated by the perpetrator in its smallest detail. As is expected in any rape, Florentino is desperate to know the identity of the violating mistress. It is interesting to note that the object of the rape, a male, feels gratitude. This version of rape, which inverts the structure of oppression in which the victim hates the perpetrator, is also observed in a female character. Leona Cassiani, like Florentino Ariza, is also raped in the novel. The circumstances for them both are similar. The victim is taken by surprise, the clothes are ripped off, and, in a forceful, frenetic fashion, he or she is raped. Florentino Ariza never sees the face of his perpetrator, nor does Leona Cassiani. However, both Florentino and Leona long to see that person again. Leona Cassiani goes on to say that she could recognize him in a crowd of a thousand men because of his shape and size and his way of making love (313). Leona spends years looking for him, not to turn him in to the authorities but to love him.

García Márquez not only inverts, but also subverts, the traditional way of looking at rape. The inversion comes from having women rape men, and the subversion by changing the feeling of hate into one of love. Neither Leona Cassiani nor Florentino Ariza develops a form of hatred of the opposite sex, as is expected to occur with rape. In fact, the two of them triumph in their own right and fall in love with each other. Leona, however, is the stronger of the two. While it is true, according to feminist author Simone de Beauvoir, that "all oppression creates a state of war" (717), the war that these two fight is one of self-growth, self-love, and self-respect.

In *Love in the Time of Cholera* the female characters are active beings in control of their own lives. There is no need to change from oppressed to oppressor, as some feminists would want, because there is no feeling of inferiority among the women characters. As the tone of the novel is ruled by love, the women do not have to dominate the men in order to defend themselves. There is no room for what Naomi Wolf calls "victim feminism" because there is no hatred within the female characters. In victim feminism, women look at themselves as weak beings, subjugated by men, and therefore must deny and attack the values and truths of what might be considered patriarchal. The women characters of *Love in the Time of Cholera* do not show such a reaction. In achieving economic independence (a basic feminist principle), none of the female characters resorts to victim feminism. Victim feminism, states Naomi Wolf, "depends on influence or persuasion rather than on seeking clout in a straightforward way" (Wolf 136). Tránsito Ariza, a single parent and Florentino's mother, manages to single-handedly buy and restore a colonial house, run a small private business, and even lend money to the rich. In addition, she spends time with Florentino, sharing with him her love for reading. The best example of a triumphant woman and the antithesis of victim feminism is Leona Cassiani. She is, without a doubt, a self-made woman. Black, young, and pretty, she is first taken for a prostitute. However, what she wants is employment. The head of personnel at the River

Company of the Caribbean, where Florentino works, gives her the lowest-level job, and Leona Cassiani performs that job with seriousness, modesty, and dedication for three years (222). Meanwhile, driven by self-pride and obvious self-assurance, she studies English at home and takes an evening class in typing. This ambition comes from a woman whose only formal education is elementary school and the School of Millinery (where one learns to make hats). Her determination pays off; Leona Cassiani eventually becomes economically independent, a homeowner, socially active, and the personal assistant to Leo XII, president-owner of the River Company of the Caribbean. Florentino Ariza falls in love with her, but the night he declares his love, she answered "it was too late" (207). From that night on, "Florentino Ariza understood at last that it is possible to be a woman's friend and not go to bed with her" (227). This exemplifies the right of exercising complete control of one's sexuality and the right to be heard, two valued aspects of feminist theory. The female characters of *Love in the Time of Cholera* (some more than others) all have a voice of their own and control over their bodies, and they all look at themselves as subjects. Women like Fermina Daza, Leona Cassiani, and the Widow Nazaret are all capable of breaking away from the state of affairs they are in—the social order in which they are born. They manage to overcome inner conflict and even trauma in order to live a life of fulfillment and, better yet, a life where the love they feel rules.

Love in the Time of Cholera fares well under a feminist reading because it vindicates the possibilities of women triumphing over the prejudices of age, race, and social class. There are instances of violence against women and women who are voiceless and weak, common traits of patriarchal writing, but those instances are not the focus of the novel; they are peripheral. They confirm the fact that, although both males and females have the possibility to overcome everything and anything before them, there are obstacles that not all can surpass. Just as Jeremiah Saint-Amour committed suicide to keep his promise of never getting old, so does América Vicuña, who is young and beautiful and leaves no note. However, their deaths seem to reaffirm the thirst for love of Fermina and Florentino.

ROBERTO GONZÁLEZ-ECHEVARRÍA

Love in the Golden Years

Since *One Hundred Years of Solitude* appeared in 1967, Gabriel García Márquez has endured having every new book of his compared to that masterpiece. He has done rather well since then, publishing in 1972 *Innocent Eréndira*, a collection of stories that alone should assure him of a place of honor in modern Latin American literature, as well as three important novels: *The Autumn of the Patriarch* (1975), *Chronicle of a Death Foretold* (1981), and *Love in the Time of Cholera* (1985). (I am referring, of course, to the date of the original publication of these books, not the date in which their English translations appeared.) These are excellent books, sharing in those qualities that have come to characterize García Márquez's fiction: a freshness in theme and form that is never obtrusive to the average reader and surprises even the most jaded critic; a style that is always playful yet able to carry heavy symbolic messages; and the presence of questions of universal relevance that issue out of everyday situations in remote Latin American towns. Comparing these novels to *One Hundred Years of Solitude* is unfair to García Márquez. To his credit, each, while unquestionably his, is different from the other and from his previous work, and excels for reasons of its own. Of the three, *Love in the Time of Cholera* may very well be the best.

If the truth be told, when it became known that García Márquez was writing a novel that centered on a senior citizen's passionate affair, many of

From *Yale Review* 85, Issue 1 (Spring 1989). © 1989 *Yale Review*.

his friends and admirers thought that he had finally gone around the bend, and hoped that he would give up and try another topic. It was one thing to write a novel about a centenarian dictator who outlives even the pleasures of power, but it was another altogether to make appealing an erotic passion between septuagenarians. The idea was certainly new, but it seemed to border on the loony. Yet, from the very first page, most of us were convinced that García Márquez had foiled us again, that he had created a unique book against all odds and expectations, that he had managed to be original while dealing with that most worn of literary topics: love. Much of that originality stems from the very fact that the novel culminates in a love affair between two old people whose bodies, ravaged by time, are not like those of the young who traditionally suffer the delights of passion in literature.

But, of course, *Love in the Time of Cholera* is not only about a crepuscular affair; it covers a wide range of amorous situations spanning over fifty years of Latin American life, from the last decades of the nineteenth century to the first two or three of the twentieth. The passion between Florentino Ariza and Fermina Daza with which the book begins and concludes merely constitutes the framework within which these characters spend almost their entire lives; the rest of the book includes many other adventures. Florentino falls in love with Fermina when they are barely teenagers, and laboriously observes the nearly medieval courtship ritual demanded by Latin American society until very recently: he writes her bundles of letters, memorizes volumes of poetry, shadows her house at all hours, faces up to the menacing opposition of her father, promises her undying love for all time (he means it). Florentino is ultimately rejected. Fermina has learned to love him at a distance and accepts his promises, but when she sees him after a trip that her father has arranged so that she will forget the impecunious young man, she decides to drop him. Up close he does not quite match the image she has formed of him through their hot exchange of letters, telegrams, and furtive messages. Fermina marries instead Dr. Juvenal Urbino, a prominent citizen of the town, through whom her father plans to fulfill his social ambitions. The novel recounts Fermina's and Juvenal's fifty years of marriage—a marriage ended by the doctor's fatal fall from a treetop while trying to recapture his polyglot parrot—and the variegated love affairs with which Florentino occupies himself while waiting for a second chance with Fermina. In that fifty-year interval Florentino becomes a man of substance, rising to the presidency of his uncle's riverboat company, in the hope that he can become worthy of Fermina.

When the doctor dies, Florentino resumes his courtship, manages to seduce Fermina, and embarks with her in one of his boats. When they reach the end of the line, Florentino orders the captain to transfer all the other passengers to another boat and to fly the yellow flag indicating that the ship is quarantined because of an outbreak of cholera on board. The lovers steam back down to their town, but when they reach it they decide not to disembark, and order the captain to sail up and down the river forever while they enjoy their love.

These are the bare bones of the plot. This is a novel rich in details, perhaps too rich in details, which convey through their meticulousness the sluggish passage of the fifty years between the breakup and resumption of Fermina's and Florentino's relationship. The lengthy plot does not follow a conventional linear progression. The novel begins on Pentecost Sunday 1929, the day on which Dr. Urbino and his friend and chess opponent, the family photographer Jeremiah de Saint-Amour, die: the first, as we saw, by accident; the second, by suicide at age sixty, a measure he had planned to take for many years to avoid the infirmities of old age. The novel then reaches back fifty years to Florentino's first sight of Fermina, laboriously narrates their courtship and split, and then inches forward to return to the day of the doctor's death and the resumption of Florentino's courtship. The way in which the plot is organized suggests that all of adult life is nothing but an annoying interruption of true love. This idea may very well be the theme of the whole novel.

Soon after her marriage to Dr. Juvenal Urbino, Fermina Daza realizes that she does not really love him, in spite of his charm, success, and elegance. She spends the next fifty years complying sedulously with the expectations that accompany her new social status, raising their children, and learning to respect the doctor, who is a model husband except for one escapade late in life. García Márquez delights in portraying the barrenness of bourgeois life, the tedium of social rituals, and the gradual decline of physical strength. *Love in the Time of Cholera* is a human comedy, neither as somber as Balzac's nor as harsh as Flaubert's, set in provincial Latin America. García Márquez's muse is more comic but no less profound. His perspective on life is more Cervantian in this respect, a rare combination of melancholy and wit. The portrayal of Juvenal Urbino is a case in point. The doctor devotes his life to his patients and to improving the general health of the town, mainly by eradicating the periodic outbreaks of cholera epidemics, one of which killed his father. The rest of his energies are spent playing chess with Saint-Amour, reading French literature, and teaching his parrot to speak French and Latin. Juvenal loves Fermina, but the stifling regularity of their lives drives them apart. There are no explosive disagreements but rather many mindless squabbles over insignificant issues. (There is a magnificent passage describing an argument they have about whether or not there is soap in the bathroom.) When the doctor dies chasing the parrot, it is as if he had finally realized that the colorful, anarchic animal that could shout the most outrageous things was his true self, a self that, significantly, was not within him but that he could not let get away.

García Márquez is not simply criticizing marriage in general, or Latin American marital customs in particular (one might add here that he has been married to Mercedes, to whom he dedicates the book, for over thirty years). *Love in the Time of Cholera* is about the incompatibility of love and social convention, the conflict between desire and social life. If, in this book, Latin American courtship appears medieval in its rituals, it is because it is based on a courtly conception of love for which conventionality is anathema. Ultimately love is love of love itself, not the desire for its actual attainment in the world. Passion is its own object. Pitted against such an impossible ideal, any social form becomes an impediment, and all of life, down to its most trivial elements, a deflection or deferment of desire. Courtly love is, at this level, a critique of all social forms, because all convention or institutionalization obstructs love's ultimate goal, which is to forestall death.

Florentino Ariza spends the fifty years after his rejection making himself worthy of Fermina, like a true courtly lover, while engaging in myriad affairs with a wide variety of women. He loves merry widows, spinsters, married women, teenage girls, women from all social classes, and lives for a while in a house of ill repute. Florentino, in short, practices nearly all the permutations of clandestine love. He finds that beneath the façade of proper behavior, there is an erotic subworld where conventions are shunted aside, and where virtue, to remember La Rochefoucauld, is nothing more than vice disguised. This underworld is ruled solely by desire and dissimulation. Florentino's affairs illustrate the strategies men and women have devised to sidestep the obstacles civilization creates to defer, deflect, or stifle love. As Florentino grows older he learns that love is the only truth, that everything else is designed to prevent its satisfaction or mask its power. It is as if with age he and his partners gradually shed social restraint, as if age functions as a boundary beyond which convention cannot survive, and which, once crossed, leads to a freedom that could only be imagined before. Rather than impeding love, age, a natural corrosive of the social fabric, appears to stimulate it. But while it may act as an incentive, physical decay is also an obstacle, a threat of destruction that is paralleled by the devastation of the world around the lovers.

Love in the Time of Cholera is a novel with an ecological subtheme. The abundant nature that surrounds the town is caught in a process of irreversible decay. Alligators, manatees, monkeys, and birds disappear from the jungle; toward the end, the riverboats have difficulty finding enough wood for their boilers. While the political urgency of this topic is clear, cosmic decline in

Love in the Time of Cholera has a different meaning and is linked to the theme of the interruption of love discussed before. There is a clear contrast between Saint-Amour's suicide and the protracted love life of Florentino Ariza, but it is a contrast that conceals a profound affinity. Saint-Amour kills himself to preserve his body from decay, to fix its image, as it were, through death. The method of his suicide, the inhalation of gold cyanide, one of the acids he uses in developing pictures, introduces to the reader an important leitmotif, almost a subplot, that takes up the topic of decay, both of the lovers' bodies and of the cosmos. This subplot has to do with alchemy, one of García Márquez's favorite subjects, and also involves cholera, the most visible destroyer of bodies in the novel.

Alchemy, as we all know, is the chemistry of the Middle Ages. Its purpose was to turn the baser metals into nobler ones like silver and preferably gold. The practice of alchemy consisted of a series of assays by which the base metals were to be melted down and turned into gold. Alchemists believed in the unity of all matter, which permitted decomposition and recomposition. The special components of metals, sulfur and mercury, endowed them with specific properties. The number of metals was usually limited to seven, corresponding to astrological principles. They formed a hierarchy, culminating in the mythical perfection of gold. The base metals were considered imperfect and lacking, as though suffering from a kind of illness for which the philosophers' stone was the cure. Alchemists sought to break down substances, to refine and make them subtle, and to transmute them through reconstitution. The most important operations were sublimation (applying heat to a dry substance to effect evaporation and adhesion to the vessel), distillation (extracting a liquid drop by drop), calcination (pulverizing a dry substance in a liquid), coagulation (reconstituting a dry substance from a liquid), fixation (rendering a volatile substance heat-resistant), and ceration (softening a substance that could not be melted). The last phases of the alchemist's work—producing the philosophers' stone and projecting it on base metals—are pure thought experiments and are generally couched in obscure and puzzling language. In fact, the whole of alchemy is a complex system of tropes that has often been incorporated into works of literature, both medieval and modern. The physical transmutations produced by love can be thought of as the equivalents of the alchemical operations; their correspondence to the planets and to astrological symbols would then assemble a vast allegory encompassing the entire cosmos. If all matter is one, then reconstitution is possible; the cosmos can be saved by rearranging its elements. Alchemy, like love, would—through heat, perhaps—seek to guide all transmutations of matter toward the enduring perfection of gold, safe from the disease of time.

In the courtly-love tradition there are degrees of perfection attainable through suffering. *Love*'s labor, like alchemy's, is to generate perfection and permanence.

Saint-Amour's suicide, it is now clear, involves the alchemical technique of evaporation. His intention, as we saw, was to preserve his body, and he does so by the use of this metal. As in a photograph, he has given permanence to his physical presence by means of gold. Gold as well as allusions to alchemy proliferate in the novel. I do not have the space to inventory all of them here, but suffice it to say that, because, as a doctor, Juvenal is trained in chemistry, his perception of the world is not far removed from that of the alchemists. Gold is present in many guises. Fermina and the doctor have just celebrated their golden anniversary as the novel begins, and the doctor dies chasing his parrot, the Spanish word for which is *loro*, very close to *l'oro, el oro*, that is to say, "gold." Florentino, spurned by Fermina for a wealthier man, sets out on a mad adventure to rescue a sunken treasure, in a clear and premonitory association of alchemy and love. While living in the whorehouse he overhears a client talk about the treasure: "The story astounded him, but he did not think of it again until a few months later, when his love awakened in him an overwhelming desire to salvage the sunken treasure so that Fermina Daza could bathe in showers of gold. Years later, when he tried to remember what the maiden idealized by the alchemy of poetry was really like, he could not distinguish her from the heartrending twilights of those times." Although he is never able to literally shower Fermina with gold or to turn her body to gold, metaphorically both Florentino and Fermina attain that state of perfection. In their final journey, Florentino and Fermina reach the port of La Dorada (the Golden One), where they decide to get rid of the other passengers and remain in the suspended time of the riverboat, enjoying their passion forever. The alchemical subplot reaches its climax as the novel ends: all the transmutations have led toward the purification of life so that only love endures in golden perfection. The final triumph is an ironic one. Fermina and Florentino will remain isolated from the coarser elements of life by allowing their love to be disguised as cholera. The quarantine is really against love, the sickness that society will in fact not tolerate, but that saves the characters from extinction, along with the manatees, the alligators, and the monkeys. Here age is of no consequence; the physical has been transmuted and preserved by gold, like Saint-Amour's body by death.

García Márquez has turned upside down one of the recurring themes of modern literature since Rousseau: youth, the tabula rasa upon which fresh symbols, new meanings, and new values will emerge; Adam naming things in the Garden, in the dawn of social and individual life. In *Love in the Time of*

Cholera, *The Autumn of the Patriarch*, and other stories, García Márquez has found, instead, that old age is a more radical vantage point, one from which all of life, all the constraints of life, appear whole, complete, and discardable; a point from which, freed from anxieties for the future, men and women can pursue whatever interests them most. In this, as in much else, he has looked back to Cervantes, whose most famous hero embarked on his notorious adventures when he was well past the blush of youth, with the freedom to defy convention that both age and madness granted him. *Love in the Time of Cholera*, García Márquez's latest masterpiece, is not only a great book, but one of the few optimistic ones to have come along in many years.

GENE H. BELL-VILLADA

The Novelist of Love

*L*ove in the Time of Cholera is García Márquez's most extensive narrative—five hundred pages in the Bruguera edition. Of its six unnumbered chapters, the final one occupies a fifth of the entire novel and is by itself longer than all of *Chronicle of a Death Foretold*. On many counts the book comes as a surprise. It is in some ways a good old-fashioned love story (as the phrase goes), a fact established in the title, which Hispanic readers in conversation habitually shorten simply to *El amor*. (We in turn shall abbreviate it *Love*.)

The book is also an intentional return to nineteenth-century realism, the outright fantasy we associate with García Márquez now being mostly absent. Among the few clear-cut exceptions are the ill-omened, colorful parrot that can speak French and Latin and even bark like a mastiff, and the forlorn ghost of a woman waving her handkerchief from the riverbank at passing ships. The narrative geography is thickly textured with descriptions worthy of Balzac, and the unnamed city in which the action unfolds is clearly modeled after the lovely, stately colonial town of Cartagena, with its old viceroys' quarter and cobblestoned streets.

At the same time the city has aspects of Barranquilla and Santa Marta,[1] for instance, the mention of a visit by aviator Charles Lindbergh, who on a 1929 goodwill tour of South America made a stop in Barranquilla (not Cartagena). Still, when the Urbinos go on their ballooning trip, Cartagena is

From *García Márquez: The Man and His Work* by Gene H. Bell-Villada. © 1990 The University of North Carolina Press.

the only place described not in terms of a site that "they flew over" but rather as one that "they could see" (*A*, 330; *L*, 226). In addition there are invented landmarks—the Gospel Park and the Arcade of the Scribes (where Florentino respectively reads poetry books and writes amorous missives for unliterate lovers), and also such imagined towns as San Juan de la Ciénaga and Puerto Padre.[2] On the other hand, the long boat journey up the Magdalena River seems true to the different stops familiar to a lonely adolescent Gabo of 1940, including the terminus at La Dorada, where one caught the train to Santa Fe (as Bogotá used to be known).

The action covers approximately sixty years, from circa 1875 to circa 1935. Fermina Daza is thirteen when she starts her first, secret engagement to Florentino, aborted three years hence. Not too long afterward, she and her newlywed husband depart on their honeymoon journey and will attend the premiere of Offenbach's *Tales of Hoffmann* (1881). The day before Dr. Urbino's absurd death the couple went to see the Hollywood version of *All Quiet on the Western Front*, from 1930 but probably screened a year or so later in Colombia. Because Fermina is seventy-two when widowed and her second courtship by Florentino lasts about a year and ten months, the closing moments of the book can therefore be placed somewhere between 1933 and 1935.

The plot, again, could not be simpler: Florentino Ariza, seventeen, falls in love with Fermina Daza, and she reciprocates, if somewhat dryly. Their relationship will be broken off as a combined result of pressure from Fermina's socially ambitious father and her own mysterious caprice. She then marries Dr. Juvenal Urbino, of the old aristocracy, and slips with some effort into the role of great lady, while Florentino rises to the top of a local river-transport firm and has at least 622 love affairs. Fifty years later Dr. Urbino dies; Florentino boldly professes his enduring love to the widow; a complicated push-and-pull courtship ensues; and their love is finally consummated on a riverboat trip.

Many elements, both experiential and literary, went into the making of this García Márquez novel. It is, as we shall see, a love story with many a difference, telling not of the all-too-familiar romantic fulfillment of two youths but of a couple in their seventies (something of a first in literature). For the second larger theme in *Love in the Time of Cholera* is that of aging and its difficulties, a process not easily romanticized. García Márquez in his interviews concerning *Love* mentions having read Simone de Beauvoir's *The Coming of Age* (in the British edition, *Old Age*), and his novel is consciously and profoundly informed by the Frenchwoman's classic study of the subject.[3] *Love* narrates, as de Beauvoir first does, the physiological changes typically accompanying aging: Florentino's loss of hair and teeth in chapter 5; his broken leg from a minor fall in chapter 6; Fermina's sudden condition of deafness in one ear aboard ship; the undegradingly honest description of her bare wrinkled shoulders and froglike skin; and the general odor of human fermentation.[4] There are also the memory losses—some slightly comical, some heartrending—suffered by Dr. Urbino and by Florentino's mother Tránsito. And there is Florentino's subjective psychological sensation of seeing time pass for others without realizing that it is passing for him too (*A*, 292, 319; *L*, 199, 228), a discrepancy to which de Beauvoir dedicates many pages.[5]

At the same time *Love* dramatizes a lively debate on elderly sexuality. The eighty-one-year-old Dr. Urbino, who has found his consolation in "sexual peace," embodies an antierotic high rationalism extolled by Plato, Seneca, and other of history's wise moralists. More, the concluding chapter reveals that the Urbino couple had not made love in two decades, while their own joyless daughter Ofelia thinks love "ridiculous" in one's middle age and simply "revolting" among the elderly. All this stands in clear contrast to Florentino's unflagging sexual vigor at seventy-eight and his consummating the love of his life at that time. Florentino and Fermina serve as eloquent rebuttal to the many long-standing forms of conventional wisdom that cruelly mock eroticism in the sunset years and doggedly claim that "the idea of sexual relations ... between elderly people is deeply shocking."[6] *Love* hence joyously celebrates sex among the aged and nullifies those silly though persistent stereotypes about "dirty old men." Not accidentally, the author first got the idea for *Love* from the touching nocturnal memory of an elderly couple dancing aboard a ship, a vision he would make into the exhilarating high point of this novel.

The book of an author approaching old age, *Love* is in some ways a serene compendium of García Márquez's life experiences and wisdom. Two such experiences are worth noting for the essential raw material they provided him. The earlier Florentino–Fermina relationship is based largely on the courtship of García Márquez's own parents.[7] His father, Eligio García, played violin, as does Florentino, and the story of the telegraphic communications that kept their stubborn romance alive is preserved almost "word for word," in "rigorously historical" form, in this novel.[8] Decades later, when the author was pursuing research for the book, he chanced to find out that his septuagenarian parents "were still—at that time—making love!"[9]

The other real-life incident that had an influential impact on the author was a news item he read in the 1960s, in Mexico, about two Americans, a loving couple in their seventies, who for four decades had been meeting yearly in Acapulco, where they would frequent the same hotel and restaurants. The amour was clandestine, for they were happily married to other people, a fact that happened to become known only when a boatman murdered the couple for their pocket money.[10] Both chilling and astounding, it is one of those stories that elicits our empathy for an absurd death at the same time that, ironically, it allows us a glimpse of eroticism and romance alive and well among the world's aged. Not for nothing does the author have Fermina hear of such an incident on the radio and come close to weeping over it, further dwelling on it in her mind during the reunion with Florentino (*A*, 461; *L*, 318).

Love and aging, then, constitute the double focus of this novel, the former being present in countless ways throughout.[11] As has often been commented, there is almost every possible sort of male–female tie in *Love*—older–younger affair and vice versa, female-on-male rape and vice versa, adultery, masturbation, prostitution, jilting, crime of passion, suicide for love, conjugal affection, unconsummated sexual attraction, young love, elderly love, and a formal courtship complete with chaperone and go-between.[12] There are serenades, references to hundreds of love letters, many subtle little tricks and gestures of pursuit, and the braid of Fermina cherished by Florentino. The cheapjack pop culture of love is alluded to in copious quantities—bad poetry, tearjerker serials, the soap operas that Fermina listens to—and often parodied. The epigraph to the novel comes from "The Crowned Goddess," a love tune from the 1970s, which García Márquez dares to insert anachronistically into his narrative and—as former president López Michelsen suggested—lends a substantial role, comparable to that assigned by Proust, in his celebrated Swann–Odette amour, to the fictional sonata by Vinteuil.

At one point, commenting on an elderly Florentino's letters, a passing phrase about "el perfume de una gardenia" (*A*, 424) is an unmistakable echo of "Perfume de gardenias," one of the most renowned of *boleros*, those Caribbean love songs whose spirit permeates much of this novel. Many other lines in the book seem lifted right out of dime-novel prose or *bolero* lyrics. Dr. Urbino's dying words, "Only God knows how much I loved you" (*A*, 72; *L*, 43), would fit perfectly either in a sentimental song or a *True Confessions*-type paperback (the Latino equivalent). On more than one occasion an amorous Florentino is described as speaking under the inspiration of the Holy Ghost—to Anglo ears a farfetched notion but perfectly conceivable in Hispanic culture, where folk-Catholicism and folk-romanticism often merge. The boat on which Florentino and Fermina finally become lovers bears the appropriately "allegorical" name *Nueva Fidelidad*. And needless to say the final line in the book—Florentino's absolutely certain "Toda la vida"; "Forever"—is the well-worn conclusion to thousands of facile songs and stories, the humorous twist here being that Florentino is talking not to

Fermina but to the captain, and refers not to his love but to the comings and goings of the riverboat.

On occasions the more solemn love rituals are wickedly parodied, simply in order that they will not be taken too seriously. Three key romantic moments in *Love* become tinged with Rabelaisian ribaldry in García Márquez's hands. In the long-awaited scene in which young Fermina at last accepts from Florentino his very first letter of courtship, a bird turd happens to drop right onto the embroidery frame she employs in receiving the crucial missive (*A*, 97; *L*, 61). Three years hence her father is about to send her safely away from her lover, and Fermina hides in the bathroom where she composes for him a brief farewell note—on a square of toilet paper, which she sends along with a braid of her hair (*A*, 128; *L*, 82). As tensions mount, the spoofing turns to outright farce: when five decades later a nervous Florentino for the first time dares to drop in on Fermina, he is suddenly seized by an uncontrollable need to defecate, and rather than run the risk of spoiling this long-awaited reunion, he cuts short his visit after a few formulaic exchanges, arranging a future date (*A*, 442; *L*, 304–5). Though love and its associated forms may be celebrated in this book, they are also indulgently and outrageously satirized when necessary.[13]

As one might expect, the realist novel *Love* includes all kinds of period detail—types of carriages, literary works, Strauss waltzes, new technologies such as crank-operated telephones and that wonderful ballooning trip, and cameo appearances by Urbino's teacher Dr. Proust (father of the novelist) and by Joseph Conrad né Korzemowski, who spends several months in the unnamed town and makes a gun-running deal with a shady Mr. Daza. And there is the social fabric of the city, with its varieties of public space, and two dominant class "blocs" represented by the Social Club (aristocracy) and the Commercial Club (bourgeoisie). The three chief characters similarly embody their respective backgrounds—Dr. Urbino, with his two resonant family names, from the old colonial elite; Fermina, the beautiful scion of the new breed of rough-hewn buccaneer capitalists who seek high standing in the young republic; and Florentino, illegitimate but connected by birth to a more modern and reputable shipping enterprise that nevertheless ravages the forest environment whose populations it largely serves. There are the accounts of hacienda life with the Sánchez clan, perhaps a nod at the milieu of Isaacs's romantic novel *María*.[14] The novel's traditionally omniscient narrator also speaks as a member of the community, shifting on occasions to the use of "we" or "us" or "here" (*A*, 24, 76; *L*, 10, 45).

In preparing for the writing of *Love*, García Márquez diligently read or reread certain European realist works, among them Alessandro Manzoni's *I promessi sposi* (1840; *The Betrothed*). The classic historical novel of Italy, it tells of a young rural couple who are ready for marriage, only to find their wedding plans repeatedly thwarted by political thugs and a cowardly priest, plus riots, wars, and, especially, a bubonic plague epidemic—but are joyfully reunited some years later. García Márquez of course has always been fascinated by accounts of plagues, and he admits to having studied with particular care the corresponding episodes in Manzoni. The influence can be seen in the plot of *Love*.[15] In one instance, the chaperone Escolástica is reported as dying in the Agua de Dios "lazareto" (*A*, 123), the latter an institution that figures prominently in *The Betrothed*.[16]

An even more important influence is Flaubert's *Sentimental Education* (1869). The phrase actually appears early on in the narrative of Florentino, when we read of the affective wisdom he would achieve "at a more advanced stage of his sentimental education" (*A*, 100; *L*, 63). García Márquez admits to having first set out to emulate the French author and combine historical panorama with love story, but in time he scaled down his objectives out of concern that the public sphere would overshadow the private, as is sometimes the case with Flaubert.[17] Still, there are striking parallels between the two novels (both of which, coincidentally, were likened by some reviewers to albums of photos). *Sentimental Education* in fact starts out on a riverboat journey, during which the protagonist, Frédéric, a sensitive if undistinguished young man, falls in love at first sight with Mme. Arnoux, a charming, pure-hearted lady "who looked like the women in romantic novels," and who in her heart will respond positively to Frédéric's affections while remaining steadfastly faithful to her flighty bourgeois husband.[18]

Frédéric in turn will continue lovesick for Mme. Arnoux throughout the book, indulging many a familiar affective formula: "Every word that fell from her lips seemed to Frédéric something new, something exclusively hers"; "he was in love with everything connected with Madame Arnoux—her furniture, her servants, her house, her street."[19] At the same time, over a ten-year period Frédéric entertains unfulfilling liaisons with the vulgar if sensual courtesan Rosanette and with the stolid heiress Mme. Dambreuse. His sole true love nevertheless remains Mme. Arnoux, whom after a gap of almost two decades he will see once again, in an affectionate though unpassionate reunion, for both are now too old and disillusioned to live the sentiments of their youth. Their lovers' reunion is hence neither a consummation nor a fresh start. The similarities with *Love in the Time of Cholera*, then, are obvious—as are the differences. Whereas Flaubert's novel ends in bleak desolation, Florentino throughout all his affairs will sustain his romantic dream and succeed in making it reality. (There may also be an intended parody of the famous carriage scene in Flaubert's *Madame Bovary* when Dr. Urbino plays a little stripping game in his own coach with Hildebranda and Fermina.)

The major difference between *Love* and its nineteenth-century prototypes, however, lies in its frank descriptions of sex. The difference has to do not only with the greater sexual tolerance of our times but also the ways in which sex is dealt with in the narrative. Physical love in most nineteenth-century fiction, when it plays any role at all, usually forms part of a sordid power struggle (Balzac's *Cousin Bette*, for instance), or is an expression either of women's wiles or of male control. In García Márquez's novel, by contrast, the erotica is depicted as delectable and positive for its own sake. To put it quite simply, Florentino and his many bedmates enjoy each other without a trace of shame or guilt. Moreover, throughout *Love* it is the women who tend to take the initiative, and their aggressive, pantherlike sexuality is implicitly acclaimed rather than prudishly maligned. Even female masturbation arises in *Love*, and Fermina's adolescent cousins gleefully compare the number of times that they are able to engage in autoeroticism daily and orgasm per session.

The contrast is especially dramatic when one considers those nineteenth-century heroines—for example, Merimée's Carmen, sinful and destructive in her sultry eroticism; or Emma Bovary, a pitiful and exploited adulteress and "fallen woman"; or Dorothea Brooke or Mme. Arnoux, among whose positive attractions is the very fact that they keep their sensuality under control. In *Love*, on the other hand, female sexuality is given free expression. Not accidentally, all but one of Florentino's sexual partners are experienced women—widowed, separated, or still married. This is partly in order to reflect the Hispanic mores of the time, when premarital sex in respectable society was largely out of the question (as demonstrated in *Chronicle*), but also because the author surely intuited that pretty girls in their teens would probably not feel attracted to a sad and homely Florentino, whose look of pained melancholy is precisely what his older paramours like about him. One of the most moving moments in this novel is when Florentino and Fermina make their serene, septuagenarian love in her cabin aboard ship, an eroticism so wise and highly distilled it takes them "beyond love."

Various temporal patterns and structural symmetries—those García Márquez trademarks—have their indispensable role in shaping *Love*. As in *The Autumn of the Patriarch* and other of the author's works, the narrative starts out with a death in the "present," in this case circa 1931; a long flashback of over fifty years takes up chapters 2–4 and most of 5, the concluding pages of which then pick up on the dangling thread from chapter 1; chapter 6 now proceeds with the final courtship and romance. Concerning parallelisms, among the most important is the set of deflowerings of Florentino and Fermina, both of them in chapter 3, on his and her respective boat trips, and in each case with more experienced and aggressive sexual partners; their elderly consummation will likewise take place on board ship, three chapters and five decades hence. The opening suicide of Jérémiah de Saint-Amour, motivated not by love but by dislike of old age, is contrastively echoed, by the love suicide of América Vicuña toward the end. That the given names of both protagonists start with the same letter *f*, and that their last names each contain a striking intervocalic *z*, is an obvious linguistic fact worth passing mention.

The triangle of chief characters forms a configuration around which the novel's major themes are to revolve. The opening chapter is Dr. Urbino's, and the inevitable first impression is that he is the hero of the book. A weighty individual, he has had a brilliant career as doctor and professor; as civic leader he has performed such admirable services as starting a firemen's corps, reviving the local theater, and ridding the town of cholera epidemics. He is patrician in lineage, is used to giving orders, and is well connected— the archbishop and the governor both attend that afternoon's banquet, and upon his death there is a three-day period of official mourning, Dr. Urbino's urbane manners are impeccable. Indeed he is all manners, and in time he will strike us as a bit complacent, too sure with his European ways—with his library of acceptable French books, all uniformly leatherbound (though no Zola), his English furniture, and his lofty rationalism. Despite the hint of youth in his name "Juvenal," the good doctor—invariably referred to by his professional title—appears never to have been a young man.

In chapter 3 we find out that Dr. Urbino was among the most eligible bachelors in town, figuring in many a young woman's dreams—was, in short, the very image of a "catch." And his wedding with Fermina was one unmatched in the century. While chapter 1 gives us a portrait of the resulting elderly affection, subsequent chapters tell the history of a long, stable companionship seriously shaken just once by the doctor's inept dalliance with a black Protestant preacher's daughter. Out in society Dr. Urbino and Fermina are the picture of poise, seen usually arm-in-arm, "the two of them in perfect harmony" (*A*, 334; *L*, 229). García Márquez quite deftly evokes this public idyll as well as those inevitable small tensions in private—the discords over the husband's wetting the edge of the toilet bowl, their harsher quarrel over an absent bar of soap, and his disastrous attempt at housework at the end of chapter 5. Still, as marriages go it is a good one, the kind we might read about today in glossy magazines.

So positive is this initial portrait of the doctor's marriage—the wife first being mentioned only a third of the way into the chapter—that an unsuspecting reader might be led to think it the central focus of the novel. As one reads of the intimate history of their relationship, however, a more complex reality emerges. The doctor is many things, but a romantic person he is not—his letters to Fermina are serious and to the point, with none of Florentino's perfumed fire. When he serenades her, he hires a concert pianist to do the job; unlike Florentino, he plays no musical instrument. Most important of all, on their first night as spouses in bed he is perfectly "aware that he did not love her" (*A*, 236; *L*, 159), for theirs is a bond originating partly in Mr. Daza's opportunistic dreams and partly in the doctor's need for "a social adornment" (*A*, 216; *L*, 145). Later, to his aging wife's casual complaint of unhappiness, the wise doctor replies sententiously, "Always remember, the most important thing in a good marriage is not happiness, but stability" (*A*, 435; *L*, 300). In retrospect, then, Dr. Urbino's dying words of love seem said because they are the expected protocol—conjugally proper rather than deeply felt.

In a darker vein there is the conjugal fife as lived and perceived by Fermina, who vaguely senses herself having developed into "a deluxe servant" employed "in [Dr. Urbino's] holy service" (*A*, 323; *L*, 221). The poet Sara Noriega—a lover of Florentino's—takes an even harsher view, dismissing the grande dame as a mere "whore" who has married a man for his money (*A*, 293; *L*, 200), though the judgment is one clearly motivated by malice. An extended key passage shows a middle-aged Fermina passing in review her own many doubts and anxieties, such as her prenuptial inner questionings as to what made the doctor any more preferable to Florentino; her later seeing her spouse as "the creature of a paternal plot"; her hellish first six years' coping with certain bitter, doltish, or narrowly prejudiced in-laws; and her suspicion that her high-and-mighty husband may be a weakling at heart (*A*, 300–306; *L*, 205–9).

And indeed, the entire flashback and final aftermath constitutes—through the characters of Fermina and Florentino, and the experience of their love regained—a sustained and subtle refutation of the premises and conventional values so skillfully established and duly honored in the opening chapter of *Love*. Fermina herself, a natural rebel, will be described throughout the book as a stubbornly mulish sort who bristles at any hint of arbitrary imposition or control. Her first three utterances to young Florentino, not accidentally, are brisk commands; and even when bedding down with her sexual partners it is she who finally decides on consummation. And yet, as the author himself once noted, Fermina becomes more bourgeois than she realized.[20] In the end she fully accepts Florentino only after too many of her upper-class supports have crumbled or proved unreliable—what with scandals in the press concerning her husband and her father, the unctuous prudery of her daughter Ofelia, and her friend and confidante Lucrecia del Real del Obispo abandoning her in time of need.

Florentino for his part stands for everything that Dr. Urbino is not. Where the doctor is rationalistic, academic in tastes, and soberly anti-passion, Florentino is spontaneous and emotive, likes all romantic poetry good or bad, and will fulfill himself as a women's man (and ultimately as one woman's man).[21] Though he does rise up in his profession and becomes a successful river transport administrator, this matters to him only insofar as it will help make him worthy of Fermina. In pointed rebuttal to the to-be-arranged marriage, moreover, during that suspenseful confrontation between Florentino and Mr. Daza when the latter orders him to stay away from his daughter, Florentino counterargues, "It seems to me that she is the one who has to decide" (*A*, 126; *L*, 81). Thus besides living for love, he is ready to die for love and to defend a woman's right to choose her mate. A romantic hero in the tradition of Goethe's Werther or Constant's Adolphe, his sentimental excesses are ironically offset both by his erotic virility and by his eccentric homeliness.

The episode of Jérémiah de Saint-Amour in the opening pages is—as critics often complain—soon forgotten and never again mentioned. But it too forms part of the broad debate that runs throughout *Love*. The Afro-Frenchman calculates his suicide long beforehand, refusing to live past sixty (seventy in the English version), out of a principled opposition to aging. What we see dramatized at the end of the book, by contrast, is the possibility of genuine passion and romance in old age. In addition, Saint-Amour has a devoted lover (whom we meet but whose name we never learn), yet has kept her clandestine and steadfastly refused to let her share in his day-to-day life. His last name notwithstanding, Jérémiah de Saint-Amour is not a man for whom love is sacred. Worse, Dr. Urbino finds out that monsieur Saint-Amour was not a political refugee but an escaped convict, a fact that casts a pall over the affection in which the doctor had held him. In this fight the later suicide of América Vicuña, however tragic, takes on a certain nobility, for it is motivated by love rather than calculation, and has the virtue of honesty, unlike the enormous shadow play set up by Jérémiah.[22]

Love in the Time of Cholera shows many of García Márquez's most admirable traits—grand sweep, hints of tragedy, and robust humor—in combination with the best qualities of the nineteenth-century novels it consciously emulates—a feel for the lived textures of everyday existence, an intuitive grasp of society and its ways, and lots of good story telling. However, it also succumbs to the notorious faults of that genre, notably an overabundance of detail (of "metonymy," as theorists might say), a discursiveness that at times becomes long-winded, and, in the middle chapters particularly, a somewhat loose and episodic structure. The author's exuberant imagination often flows to excess in the pages of *Love*, such as those lengthy lists of house pets in the first chapter and of European consumer purchases in the third. And though each one of Florentino's many depicted women friends is a delight individually, the instances accumulate in sufficient numbers so as to muddy the narrative. Other, nonsexual stray episodes appear similarly gratuitous—for example, the account of Florentino's ill-fated attempt, in chapter 3, at raising a sunken Spanish galleon.

It is perhaps no paradox that *Love* is García Márquez's most joyous book—and also his least disciplined or rigorous. Yet it is a novel that stays in the mind, producing a deep and lasting glow of satisfaction *after* being read, and the outer chapters are as beautiful and artful as anything ever fashioned by the author. Moreover, García Márquez's millions of readers can only applaud his courage and originality in writing a novel of love (a subject traditionally thought of as the preserve of younger authors) when on the verge of old age, a bit like Verdi composing his single comic opera, *Falstaff*, when in his seventies. The Colombian literary wizard's capacities for independence and self-renewal inevitably move us to admiration.

NOTES

1. López Michelsen, "López presenta la novela," p. 7.

2. Ibid.

3. Simons, "The Best Years of His Life," p. 48.

4. Cf. Beauvoir, *Old Age*, the first chapter, "Old Age and Biology," pp. 17–37.

5. This is the precise focus of Beauvoir's chapter "The Discovery and Assumption of Old Age," in ibid., pp. 283–361.

6. Ibid., p. 317.

7. See chapter 3 above.

8. Arroyo, "El amor, la vejez, la muerte," p. 2. Font Castro, "Las claves reales," passim.

9. Hamill, "Love and Solitude," p. 192.

10. Simons, "García Márquez on Love," p. 23.

11. Arroyo, pp. 2–3.

12. Palencia-Roth, "La primera novela de García Márquez después del premio Nobel," p. 7.

13. In this connection it is worth recalling that Flaubert's father was a doctor, while García Márquez's had studied medicine.

14. See chapter 2.

15. Simons, "García Márquez on Love," p. 23.

16. In her otherwise fine translation, Grossman semantically narrows "lazareto" to "leprosarium" (*L*, 79).

17. Arroyo, p. 2.

18. Flaubert, *Sentimental Education*, p. 22.

19. Ibid., pp. 59 and 65–66.

20. Simons, "The Best Years of His Life," p. 48.

21. For an excellent discussion along these fines, see Minta, *Gabriel García Márquez*, pp. 138–41.

22. Ibid., pp. 142–43.

MICHAEL BELL

Not Flaubert's Parrot:
Love in the Time of Cholera

Although Márquez' next novel keeps the familiar theme of time in its title, it now gives first place to the word 'love'. It tells, in a leisurely and protracted series of flashbacks, the story of the life-long love of the illegitimate, and once poor, Florentino Ariza for Fermina Daza. Their teenage love had been sustained largely by his letters as she was sent away by her ambitious father. But when they suddenly met after this long separation, her 'illusion' of love, as she then saw it, was immediately dispelled. She rejected him to marry, although also after a period of rejection, the socially well-placed doctor Juvenal Urbino, who was already some thirty years old. Much of the book is taken up with a study of this marriage and of the myriad affairs by which Florentino tries to fill the space left by Fermina while waiting one day to possess her. The present action of the novel opens on the day of Dr Urbino's sudden death, in his eighties, while trying to retrieve his escaped parrot. His death allows Florentino to resume his courtship of Fermina. This time he is eventually successful and the story ends with them sailing up and down the Magdalena river, isolated by a cholera flag, on a boat owned by the steamship company of which Florentino is now the president. It ends, that is to say, with a romantic gesture for which it is hard to imagine the realistic outcome.

Cholera is, in short, a love story and it is handled as if the love motif of *Chronicle* had now expanded to require a book of its own. This is not just a

---

From *Gabriel García Márquez: Solitude and Solidarity* by Michael Bell. © 1993 Michael Bell.

49

matter of space, or even of narrative proportion. The love story in *Chronicle* seemed to need a different mode of fiction and part of the interest of *Cholera* is not only to develop this possibility but implicitly to reflect upon and justify it. The relationship between the two books, in other words, is a striking instance of an increasingly evident feature of Márquez' *oeuvre*. One book seems partly to give birth to another which then goes on in turn to develop such a distinctive life of its own that it represents, if not a critique of the preceding work, then a significantly new vantage point from which to see it.

Cholera is most briefly, and perhaps most adequately, described as a love story. For the homely populism of the phrase is part of the book's own characteristic note. Yet the very familiarity and apparent simplicity of this phrase, indeed its nearness to cliché, present special problems of value and attention. That is why Márquez does not just seek to tell a popular love story; he sets out at the same time a sophisticated vindication of his subject and its form. This consists largely of a sustained meditation on both terms, 'love' *and* 'story', and on the relationship between them. But Márquez also places this meditation within a wide-ranging, if implicit, context of literary history. The book is full of narrative elements which are in the first instance simply part of the action but which at the same time provide a continuous, discreet means of self-reference on the part of the fiction by which it defines and locates itself against some of the prestigious achievements, and widely accepted criteria, of earlier modern literature.

The figure who provides the significant reference point here is Flaubert, although what is strictly at stake is not so much Flaubert himself as his myth. It is Flaubert's prestigious impact on modern literary thinking and most especially his ideal of an impersonally technical control by which the ineradicable human impulse to romance is contained within an ironically detached, aestheticised nihilism. The form is inseparable from the vision. It is appropriate as well as ironic that Julian Barnes' *Flaubert's Parrot* (1984), with its witty and telling reaffirmation of the Flaubertian spirit, and its parenthetic swipe at 'magical realism', should have been published only a year before *Cholera* (1985). For *Cholera* offers a sustained, if side-long, challenge to the Flaubertian spirit.

I say 'side-long' because the direct allusions to Flaubert are the merest hints; anything more overt might have turned the novel into an elite intra-literary game rather than the popular and independently accessible work it actually is. Hence there is a passing reference to Florentino' Ariza's 'educación sentimental' / 'sentimental education'.[1] And the local hospital is named after St. Julian the Hospitaler (pp. 182, 337 / pp. 125, 234). But once our attention is focused, we notice that a character who has an intense relationship with a parrot dies looking at it. And then we see the further significance of having at the centre of the story a study of the prosaic marriage of a provincial doctor and of his wife's suppressed romanticism. Of course, Dr Urbino and Fermina are a far cry from Charles and Emma Bovary but what the marriages have in common is their mundane representativeness as pointed up by the narrative in each case. The differences in personal quality are part of the force of the comparison. These differences challenge the basis of Flaubertian representativeness just as Márquez brings a fresh light to the Flaubertian use of the cliché.

In fact, indirection characterises the book more generally than just in the sidelong relation to Flaubert. Indirection has now become its dominant technical strategy and, we might almost say, its subject matter. For the narrative constantly sneaks up on the reader just as the character's emotions are constantly taking them by surprise. It is worth pausing on this aspect of the narrative before pursuing the implication of the Flaubertian allusions.

As has been noted several times, Márquez has always used techniques of indirection. The technical devices listed by Vargas Llosa are for the most part different forms of narrative obliqueness. In *Cholera*, however, these seem even more accentuated and humorously shared with the reader. For example, a favourite Marquesian effect has always been to introduce new material as if it were already known to the reader. Even an episode as important as the massacre of the strikers in *Hundred Years* is edged into the narrative in this way. Very often the effect, as in *Hundred Years*, can be to reinforce the spatialised chronology of the narrative. The story is told as if it were already within our possession. The technique can also disguise the importance of what is being introduced. To speak of something as if we already knew all about it is to imply that the topic does not need further explanation.

In *Cholera*, Márquez is less concerned to create the compressed and mythic spatialising of time which he sought in *Hundred Years* but he is still concerned to dramatise the interrelations of emotion and time. Time both changes, and is unable to change, Florentino's love. Like the colonel of *No One Writes*, Florentino affirms a Quixotic value by his heroic endurance. At the beginning of his love for Fermina, Florentino is unaware that it will not be consummated till nearly the end of their lives; that his life is going literally to enact what would normally be a poetic hyperbole. And in a complementary way, Dr Urbino does not know at the beginning of the novel that this is to be his last day. Here Márquez reverses the device of apparently foretelling Col. Aureliano Buendía's death by firing squad. The opening chapter has several references to the doctor's death which make us suppose it to be still a long way off, as in:

> ... dictó en la Escuela de Medicina todos las días de lunes a
> sábado, a las ocho en punto, hasta la víspera de su muerte. (p. 21)

> ... he taught at the School of Medicine every morning, from
> Monday through Saturday, at eight o'clock punctually, until the
> day before his death. (p. 12)

We are unlikely at first to realise that this is the day of his death and
particularly since this account of *his* own day is being placed in evident
contrast, and in apparent narrative subordination, to that of his friend, the
aptly named Jeremiah de Saint-Amour, who has foretold and arranged his
own death for that very day. In the same opening chapter, Dr Urbino's 'wife'
and the parrot are also introduced with a comparably deceptive casualness.
We do not know what principally to focus on in this opening chapter, just as
the characters do not know what is going to prove most important in their
lives. The whole narrative unfolds in a comparably ambiguous way creating
a curious effect of leisurely suspense or suspenseful leisure. The central love
affair is finally developed only at the very end of the novel and depends
entirely on this anterior effect of constant distraction. The main body of the
book is a narrative *tour de force* in simply filling the space between youth and
age. In the abstract, this formula is a Beckettian one, but the Marquesian
emphasis is on the preciousness rather than the emptiness of time. The
book's delight in its own narrative bravura enacts its theme of enjoyment.

The mixture of suspense and leisure in the narrative is in the first
instance, therefore, a way of enforcing a *carpe diem* recognition. But it does
so by constantly revealing the processes by which everyday life blunts and
distracts from this romantic wisdom. Proust saw habit as the great deadener.
Márquez' narration constantly enacts an enjoyment of the momentary
texture of experience while tripping us up if we are not on the alert for
sudden changes. In this respect it reflects the emotional lives of the
characters. The emotional life is volatile and it is overlaid with habit and
rationalisation so that its subterranean current is often undetected. Or else
when this does come to the surface, it is not understood. Fermina's response
to her disgraced father's death is a case in point:

> Fermina Daza no pudo reprimir un suspiro de alivio cuando le
> llegó la noticia de la muerte, y no le guardó luto para evitar
> preguntas, pero durante varios meses lloraba con una rabia sorda
> sin saber por qué cuando se encerraba a fumar en el baño, y era
> que lloraba por el. (pp. 308–9)

> Fermina Daza could not repress a sigh of relief when the news of
> his death came and in order to avoid questions she did not wear
> mourning, but for several months she wept with dumb fury
> without knowing why when she locked herself in the bathroom to
> smoke, and it was because she was crying for him. (p. 215)

As has been seen in several previous works, Márquez frequently withholds
omniscient insight into his characters. In this book he suggests more
directly the unknowability of true feeling to simple introspection and the
corresponding impossibility of summing up a relationship. This
recognition is crucial to the portrayal of the Urbinos' marriage. Apart from
anything else, the novel is a remarkable, if humorous, treatment of
marriage but it is so because this marriage, and marriage in general, are
both understood in the light of this fundamental recognition. In *Chronicle*,
the narrator engaged the difficulty of understanding the mentality of a
different culture. To an important extent, every long-term marriage
develops its own culture which no outsider can ever be sure to have
penetrated.

From one point of view the marriage of Dr Urbino and Fermina is
merely a fifty-year interruption of Florentino's courtship. And the flashback
technique of the narrative frankly treats it as such. Yet it also proves to be the
route, and perhaps the necessary route, to the final romance, since both
characters develop importantly through their experiences during this period.
It is the marriage that gives Fermina her realistic appreciation of romance.
And from this point of view it is important that the story should give the
marriage its proper weight. It is not merely an obstacle. What we most come
away with is a sense of its absolute resistance to any summary statement of
its emotional quality or success. It is a very average sort of a marriage seen
with clear, but not cynical, eyes. The relationship has been passionate,
affectionate, boring, angry and desperate. But none of these sums it up. It
presents no easy counter-term to the subsequent romance and it thereby
gives a greater force, and testing, to the romance when it comes. In this
novel, of course, the counter-term to 'romance' is not 'marriage' but 'age'. As
the title suggests, the lovers triumph over time.[2]

In acknowledging this weight and complexity in the Urbinos'
marriage, Márquez is affirming such a significance in marriage *per se*. For
the specific internal chemistry of the Urbinos' marriage suggests something
about the nature of marriage at large. In the classic tradition of romantic
love, passion was necessarily adulterous.[3] Marriage has always for that
reason been a central theme of the novel because it represents the point of
tension, for good or ill, between personal fulfilment and the requirements

of the social order. That was the structural function of marriage in the nineteenth-century novel of which *Madame Bovary* is a classic instance.[4] But in this connection it is suggestive that, whereas Flaubert's title *Madame Bovary* refers to the former Emma Roualt purely by her married name, Fermina Daza, partly because of the different Hispanic conventions, continues to be referred to in the narrative by her personal and maiden names. In the twentieth century marriage has become more a matter of personal fulfilment, or otherwise, with less weight given to its meaning as a social institution. But wherever such a modern marriage continues to represent a lifetime commitment, it can actually embody the workings of the reality principle even more strongly and subtly than did the old sense of a social institution.

For the social institution represented an impersonal order to which an individual would give a personal inflection but which individuals did not create and could not significantly modify. The institution itself could therefore be held responsible for the happiness or otherwise of those inside it. But with the progressive weakening of the social institution, marriage has acquired an almost unique value in being a closed system in which two individuals live with the continuing, direct consequences of their own personalities. A lifetime's career in teaching, for example, may wreak untold damage, if only that of wasted time, on generations of students, but the perpetrator may remain happily unconscious because the students continually go away. Any comeback is only temporary. In a marriage, by contrast, the comeback is both short-term and long-term; it expresses itself at varying levels of consciousness; and above all it is inescapable as long as the marriage lasts.

The Urbino's marriage lasts into the new century and Márquez' presentation of it catches this intimate working of the reality principle as the interaction of two individuals defining and creating each other within a closed system. His humour brings out the structural dimension of this as well as the immediately personal, and often painful, feeling. At the same time, of course, the humour is a distancing device. The marriage is not the ultimate subject of the book. But he nonetheless communicates the rounded and complex workings of a marriage with an insider's knowledge in a way that I doubt Flaubert could. Flaubert could understand it very well in his own way, which was as an outsider. The bachelorhood of Flaubert is as relevant to his literary vision as is that of James or Turgenev. And by the same token, Márquez' own long marriage seems to have been an importantly formative precondition of his imaginative world just as, more obviously, D. H. Lawrence's was. Of course, this is not simply to attribute all such effects to marriage *per se*. It depends on the individuals' being open to its possibilities.

If Flaubert had married he would undoubtedly, like many another, have remained essentially a bachelor and he was wise not to inflict this fate on a woman. That was part of the sense in which he *did* understand the question very well from his own point of view.

There is something larger at stake, therefore, in the volatility of the Urbino marriage in contrast to the enclosure of the Bovary's. Of course, in an immediate sense the two marriages are incomparable because the authors are writing about different characters and for different purposes. But in a more significant underlying sense the characters are precisely the products of these different artistic and personal visions. With his French suspicion of feeling and romance, Flaubert sardonically traces the inextricability of the romantic impulse in the lives of his major characters and implicitly identifies its only proper expression as being in the art of the book itself. Márquez has a more English sense of the necessary, and proper, interaction of feeling and world so that the important question is rather to discriminate the quality of the feelings. It is as if Márquez were seeking to write something more like an English novel of moral and emotional growth while staying within Flaubert's terms. Only in this way could he make fully conscious and pertinent the challenge to the Flaubertian spirit. Henry James once remarked, after one of his visits to Flaubert's literary circle, how no one present was aware that George Eliot's *Daniel Deronda* had just been published and how none of them would have understood the significance of the event if they had been told of it.[5] Hence Márquez deliberately invokes Flaubert's terms and not least by keeping the general categories of 'reality' and 'romance' distinct in the reader's mind.

The text is at all times humorously aware both of the fundamental struggle between romance and reality and of their inextricability. This is apparent in the young Florentino's business letters:

> ... Florentino Ariza escribía cualquier cosa con tanta pasión, que hasta los documentos oficiales parecían de amor. Los manifiestos de embarque le salían rimados por mucho que se esforzara en evitarlo, y las cartas comerciales de rutina tenían un aliento lírico que les restaba autoridad. (p. 246)

> ... Florentino Ariza would write anything with so much passion that even official documents seemed to be about love. His bills of lading came out in rhyme however he tried to avoid it, and routine business letters had a lyrical air that undermined their authority. (p. 171)

And this initial statement of the theme is answered much later when the mature Florentino begins to have some success in wooing the widowed Fermina with a different kind of letter:

> Era una carta de seis pliegos que no tenía nada que ver con ninguna otra que hubiera escrito alguna vez. No tenía ni el tono, ni el estilo, ni el soplo retórico de los primero años del amor, y su argumento era tan racional y bien medido, que el perfume de una gardenia hubiera sido un exabrupto. En cierto modo, fue la aproximación más acertada de las cartas mercantiles que nunca pudo hacer. (p. 424)

> It was a six-page letter, quite unlike any he had ever written before. It did not have the tone, the style, or the rhetorical air of his early years of love, and his argument was so rational and measured that the scent of a gardenia would have been out of place. In a way, it was his closest approximation to the business letters he had never been able to write. (p. 296)

While we see that Florentino has changed, the continuity of the business letter theme allows us also to see that this later style is only a transposition of the same melody. The youthful romance is not transcended so much as transformed.

Márquez enjoys tracing the all-pervading nature of romance whereby it constantly subverts and assimilates its apparent opposites. At one point, as his lover Angeles Alfaro, the young girl who plays the cello naked, leaves on the boat for good, Florentino comes to recognise that 'se puede estar enamorado de varias personas a la vez, y de todas con el mismo dolor, sin traicionar a ninguna' (pp. 393–4) / '... one can be in love with several people at the same time, and feel the same anguish for each, without betraying any of them' (p. 274) Whereupon he remarks as a general dictum: '"El corazón tiene más cuartos que un hotel de putas"' / 'The heart has more rooms than a whorehouse'.[6] He is momentarily shocked by this recognition but the narrative is not and, sure enough, '... no bien había desaparecido el barco en la línea de la horizonte, cuando ya el recuerdo de Fermina Daza había vuelto a ocupar su espacio total' / '... no sooner had the ship disappeared over the horizon, than the memory of Fermina Daza once again filled all his space'. Romantic love, it has already been remarked, is not essentially an ethical impulse. As Stendhal bluntly put it: 'True passion is a selfish thing'.[7] The remark about the heart and the whorehouse is an earthy way of putting what the narrative at large seems to bear out: that love is resilient, elastic, volatile and multiple. The image is even perhaps a distant cousin of 'My Father's house has many mansions' and it is worth remarking in passing that the acceptance of multiplicity is an artistic, as well as a psychological, principle. The solitude of Melquiades, and of the 'lonely God' of *In Evil Hour*, arose not from the absence, so much as the even-handed multiplicity, of their relations with humankind at large.

That at least is the more negative side of the equation. But this book constantly suggests the more positive interrelations of 'love' and 'fiction' which may lurk in the common expression 'love story'. Love may be an archetypal subject of fiction partly because it has a strong element of the fictional in its own constitution. Hence, where the anti-romantic tradition from Cervantes through Flaubert to Nabokov has used the elements of fiction to expose romance, Márquez rather delights in the inextricable working of the fictional within love. Florentino, for example, becomes a scribe of love, drawing on his own feelings to compose love letters for others. He then finds himself conducting both sides of a correspondence which leads to a marriage and a child. This is the opposite joke to Flaubert's construction of a love conversation between Emma Bovary and Leon out of the clichés he sardonically amassed for his *Dictionary of Received Ideas*. In the case of Márquez' young couple, at least for all we know to the contrary, the genuineness of the feeling overrides and survives the artificiality of the occasion. The difference is partly an acceptance of language, even popular and clichéd language, as being independent of the feeling invested in it rather than as necessarily debasing the feeling in the expression. In so far as it remained within the Flaubertian orbit, much modern literature showed an unassuagable nostalgia for the genuinely popular touch. Joyce placed the common man at the centre of his work but could not be said simply to write for him. Márquez, for all his patrician spirit, has increasingly sought the popular note. This book is his most striking attempt to square the circle; to write a genuinely popular and accessible romance while maintaining, if only to challenge, the sophistication of a high modernist consciousness.

So, for example, as the final romance develops, Fermina becomes a fan of soap operas; a genre well known for its naïve equivocation with real life and its tendency to identify the performers with their parts. With a typical Marquesian effect, she listens to these interspersed with the real news which is how she hears the report of the elderly couple whose murder reveals them to have been clandestine lovers for forty years despite their each having a stable and fruitful marriage. The news item reduces Fermina to tears as the soap operas, which are designed to play on the feelings, do not, for it is in the fate of this couple that Fermina and Florentino recognise their potential selves. By intermingling the 'real' world of his fiction with that of soap opera,

Márquez is not merely endorsing his heroine's love of soap operas, he is presenting his own story as a superior version of the genre. Superior, that is to say, but not condescending. Soap opera may be an undemanding form but Márquez feels no need to distance himself from it for the points of commonality are ultimately much greater than those of difference. In the 1980s Márquez was increasingly fascinated by the potential power of this phenomenally popular form. As he says, more people watch a soap opera in one night than have ever read his books.[8]

In short, Márquez is writing a popular romance which seeks to vindicate itself with a sophisticated literary historical self-consciousness. He fully acknowledges the projective and illusory nature of romantic love, what Stendhal called 'crystallisation'.[9] The teenage love of Fermina and Florentino is ended abruptly when she suddenly sees his prosaic reality close up and feels 'el abismo del desencanto' (p. 155) / 'the abyss of disenchantment' (p. 106). This echoes the puzzled recognition of Proust's Swann that Odette, the object of his formerly consuming passion, was not even his 'type'. But just as Proust's novel goes on to absorb this Flaubertian recognition into a more complex aesthetic vision of 'paradise' as an imaginative construct won from time, so Florentino's obstinate persistence is to effect a comparable change in the nature of feeling through time and with the help of his fictional imagination.

Perhaps that is why Proust is mentioned, but only obliquely, in the text (p. 172 / p. 118). For although its tone and ambition are so different, this is Márquez' most Proustian novel. The Proustian experience is transposed into the key of Márquez. There were Proustian echoes, for example, in *Hundred Years* but they were seen mainly in a critical light as part of the Buendía's insidious nostalgia. In *Cholera*, on the other hand, romantic nostalgia is more sympathetically treated and indeed the increasing nostalgia of Fermina for her youth even before being newly won over by Florentino is an important, unconscious step towards their late-flowering love. Without the elaborate metaphysics of love and imagination through which Proust constructs his final paradisal vision, their late affair has a comparable basis in recovered emotion and a consciously challenging transcendence of immediate reality. And likewise, as with Proust, there has been a conscious quest for the romantic experience on the part of the central male character while the true route to that experience proves to have been a process taking place largely outside of consciousness or will.

Márquez' carefully considered privileging of the romantic experience is further offset by his chosen counter-term of 'cholera'. Throughout his *oeuvre* Márquez has used the technique of parenthetical reference which Vargas Llosa calls the 'caja china' or Chinese box. In other words, he imparts crucial information *a propos* of something else. In the early novellas especially, the horrors of the political situation were commonly revealed in this casual way, as in the remark that the funeral at the beginning of *No One Writes* was the first death by natural causes in ten years. The effect of this technique as used earlier was, of course, to increase our sense of such horrors. The present novel is likewise full of references to the civil wars and, one might think, the more tellingly so in so far as these references extend throughout the long lifetimes of the principal characters. But the actual effect is the reverse of this. We are rather struck by how little the essential lives of these characters are affected by political conditions and the long-standing nature of these conditions makes them appear to be rather one of the immovable conditions of life. This seems to be the principal function of the cholera motif. It metaphorically absorbs references to civil violence into a natural scourge; a scourge that might ideally be cured but is primarily to be understood as an aspect of the human condition at large. If this particular condition were removed, that is to say, the general nature of human existence would not be significantly altered. The supreme value of love would still be subject to time and mortality. This is the viewpoint from which Florentino's 'indiferencia política rayaba los límites de lo absoluto' (p. 388) / 'indifference to politics approached the limits of the absolute' (p. 270). Love, in short, will always be in the time of cholera; an implication which is clearer in the Spanish title where the 'times' of cholera are in an indefinite and recurrent plural.

But there is a further, more intrinsic, reason for this inescapability of conditions which is that love itself stands in no simple opposition to cholera. Indeed, it promotes cholera. For if the image of cholera assimilates war to human mortality at large, it also encompasses the dangerous fever of love. Hence, when Florentino is first in love,

> ... su madre se aterrorizó porque su estado no se parecía a los desórdenes del amor sino a los estragos del cólera. (p. 97)

> ... his mother was terrified because his condition did not seem like the pangs of love so much as the ravages of cholera. (p. 65)

And late in life, as her memory became confused, she

> ... solía decir: 'De lo único que mi hijo ha estado enfermo es del cólera.' Confundía el cólera con el amor, por supuesto, desde mucho antes de que se embrollara la memoria. (p. 320)

> ... used to say: 'The only disease my son ever had was cholera.'

> She was confusing cholera with love, of course, long before her
> memory became muddled. (p. 222)

Not only is love in itself a form of cholera, but Florentino images his
courtship as a military campaign. In other words, the apparently polar
oppositions are increasingly complexified as a double action takes place. On
the one hand, cholera is a collective and distancing image for all that stands
in opposition to romance. In that respect it is potentially undiscriminating
and sentimental. On the other hand, romantic love is also part of the disease.
We have already noted that the romantic impulse is distinct from the ethical
and it should be remembered that Florentino's affairs have cost the lives of
two of the women concerned. Hence, when the lovers finally hit on the idea
of protecting their romantic isolation by sailing under the flag of cholera
there is a multilayered appropriateness in the gesture. They *are* in the grip of
a dangerous contagion.

The novel's affirmation of romance, then, is in the face not just of a hostile
or prosaic world, but of the darker side of romance itself. In this respect, the
peculiar triumph of the book is its control of tone. It affirms a permanent and
necessary impulse which it recognises can never be entirely lived and should
perhaps not be attempted. In a truer and more penetrating sense than the
phrase usually implies, this novel is a 'poem in prose'. It is not, that is to say,
written in a 'poetic' prose. Rather the poetic affirmation of romance is set
within a prose which refuses ever quite to assimilate it. As with *Chronicle*, the
meaning of the work lies in the tension between its 'poetry' and its 'prose'. I say
tension because in refusing quite to assimilate the romance it also protects it.

With a happy insight which encompasses the popular note of the book,
Michael Wood has expressed something of this double effect by referring to
this novel as Márquez' 'bolero'.[10] In his early journalism, both while he was
still based on the Caribbean coast and when suddenly removed to Bogotá, a
city incidentally whose name is actively avoided in the novel, Márquez often
wrote warmly of the popular song tradition of the coastal region. Wood's
formula catches very well the positive spirit of Márquez' popular expression
of the romantic impulse. But there is a body of musical allusion in the text of
the novel itself which reinforces the literary historical allusions and gives his
populism a challenging edge.

I have already indicated the significance of soap opera but more
importantly there are many references in the novel to the characters' love of
music and especially of opera proper. Music, for example, is supremely
important to Doctor Urbino and he raises the topic early in his courtship of
Fermina:

'Le gusta la música?'

Lo preguntó con una sonrisa encantadora, de un modo casual, pero ella no le correspondió.

'A qué viene la pregunta?' preguntó a su vez.

'La música es importante para la salud.' dijo er.

Lo creía de veras, y ella iba a saber muy pronto y por el resto de su vida que el tema de la música era casi una fórmula mágica que el' usaba para proponer una amistad, pero en aquella momento lo interpretó como una burla. (p. 178)

'Do you like music?'

'Why do you ask?' she asked in turn.

'Music is important for health,' he said.

He really believed this, and she was to know very soon, and for the rest of her life, that the subject of music was almost a magic formula that he used to propose friendship, but at that moment she took it for a joke. (p. 122)

Through Dr Urbino, Márquez introduces music as a touchstone in the book at large. Music seems to be a sustaining power of life itself even for this man whose profession is medicine. Fermina soon sympathises with this. She regularly accompanies him to the opera and the opening of *Les Contes d'Hoffmann* is one of their supreme joint memories of their honeymoon in Europe. Nonetheless, the unequal note of this opening is maintained in that the primary enthusiasm is always his. And there is a similar pattern of inequality with respect to Florentino. The great musical enthusiast in his life is his uncle, Leo XII, with 'su afición maniática por el *bel canto*' (p. 384) / 'his maniacal love of bel canto' (p. 268). Florentino sympathises with, rather than actually participates in, this taste. Hence 'se conmovió' (p. 391) / 'he was moved' (p. 272) when his uncle sang *addio alla vita* from *Tosca* to celebrate Florentino's assuming the presidency of the river boat company but he would not think to join in.

The musical references point to a realm or value that largely escapes verbal expression. This stands partly in ludicrous contrast to reality, as when uncle Leo, as a would-be Dionysus, loses his false teeth trying to impose the power of music on the creatures of the jungle. Yet it is also partly transformative as in the early incident of the concert in which Dr Urbino, having been scandalised by the revelation of his dead friend's long-standing mistress, is brought to show 'lealtad con la mujer que había repudiado cinco horas antes,' (p. 65) / 'loyalty to the woman he had repudiated five hours earlier' (p. 42). His change of heart is effected more by the influence of music than by the intercession of his wife. The whole episode of the concert plays on the interweaving of the music with the emotional and social reality of the occasion.

Music appears throughout the book as the ambivalent but indispensable power of romance. And since opera in particular is both a musical and a dramatic genre, it is obliged to spell out formally its remove from realist terms and in doing so it speaks for the novel too. What an opera might express, the novel vindicates and protects. The doubleness is embodied in the different kinds, and degrees, of musical appreciation seen in the characters. It is evident that Dr Urbino, the connoisseur and promoter of opera, has a rational and sublimative relation to it, while Florentino's uncle, in keeping with the more romantic tenor of his life, actually sings. By contrast, Fermina and Florentino are sympathetically associated with music and opera without being enthusiasts or direct participants. This is because they ultimately wish to live out its values in reality. To make it possible for them to do so, the novel adjusts its own imaginative lens, its implicit contract with the reader, by means of the opera theme.

This can be seen by the exercise of imagining a passage of Márquez verbally unchanged but understood in a Flaubertian spirit. Borges' Pierre Menard would have us read the text of *Don Quixote* to yield a modern, non-Cervantean meaning.[11] That was a difficult feat which even Menard failed to achieve. But it is relatively easy to imagine the following passage as written by Flaubert:

> La temporada se abrió con una compañía francesa de ópera cuya novedad era un arpa en la orquesta, y cuya gloria inolvidable era la voz inmaculada y el talento dramático de una soprano turca que cantaba descalza y con anillos de pedrerías preciosas en los dedos de los pies. A partir del primer acto apenas si se veía el escenario y los cantantes perdieron la voz por el humo de las tantas lámparas de aceite de corozo, pero los cronistas de la ciudad se cuidaron muy bien de borrar estos obstáculos menudos y de magnificar los memorables. Fue sin duda la initiativa más contagiosa del doctor Urbino, pues la fiebre de la ópera contaminó hasta los sectores menos pensados de la ciudad, y dio origen a toda una generación de Isoldas y Otelos, y Aidas y Sigfridos. (pp. 73–4)

The season opened with a French opera company whose novelty was a harp in the orchestra and whose unforgettable glory was the impeccable voice and dramatic talent of a Turkish soprano who sang barefoot and wore rings set with precious stones on her toes. After the first act the stage was hardly to be seen and the singers lost their voices because of the smoke from so many palm oil lamps, but the chroniclers of the city took care to erase these minor obstacles and to magnify what was memorable. Without a doubt it was Dr Urbino's most contagious initiative, for opera fever infected the most unexpected sections of the city and gave birth to a whole generation of Isoldes and Otellos and Aidas and Siegfrieds. (p. 48)

Márquez' vision here is no less ironical than Flaubert's would have been, but with a different kind of irony. In Flaubert, for example; we would know how to read the 'impeccable' voice of the Turkish soprano but in Márquez we cannot be so sure. If the 'chroniclers of the city' are adjusting their verbal lenses so, in his own way, is Márquez. Like Dr Urbino looking on the life of the same city, he loves it enough 'para verla con los ojos de la verdad' (p. 167) / 'to see it with the eyes of truth' (p. 115). Where a classic English novelist, like George Eliot, would say you can *only* see the human truth *when* looking with the eyes of love, Márquez is somewhere between that stance and the Flaubertian. And, once again, the final imagery of disease in the passage links this ambivalent complex of feeling to both the central motifs of cholera and romance. Dr Urbino, the rational and effective campaigner against the cholera, has himself been responsible for this 'contagious initiative'.

The fact that we can so readily perform the imaginary exercise of reading the passage in the spirit of Flaubert arises partly from the fact that opera has been a recurrent motif by which both realist and modernist writers have defined their own generic forms. In *Madame Bovary* itself, Emma's readiness to be emotionally caught up by a performance of *Lucia di Lammermoor* is treated with crushing irony. On the other hand, Joyce's *Ulysses*, and several consciously modernist works of Thomas Mann, not only present operatic experience in a more positive light, they use it as a partial model, or criterion, for their own conscious departures from realist form.

As a reading of Joyce, and of *Cholera* itself, reminds us, opera at the turn of the century was a highly popular form; and hence the desire of some of these earlier writers to distance themselves from it. It is significant that opera has acquired a new popularity, and a new kind of popularity, precisely over the period of Márquez' career for the late twentieth-century popularity of opera has been part of a transformation in the understanding of the form itself. That it now regularly attracts great theatrical directors reflects a more serious and integral understanding of its nature as musical drama. In the early 1960s it was possible to think of the middle part of the nineteenth century as a relatively weak period for drama. This judgement may indeed be a fair one but in making it one would now have to recognise that opera was one of the forms into which the dramatic imagination of the period went. And it could strike important notes of political feeling as was recognized by the crowds who drew Verdi's hearse through the streets singing the Israelites' chorus from *Nabucco*. That is why Márquez' late twentieth-century novel, set around the turn of the century, is able to unite in its operatic theme both the popular note of the earlier period and the generic appreciation of recent decades. A way of expressing the reservation about *Chronicle* would be to say that its love theme seemed to require the insertion of a different mode of fiction which it could only with tact and difficulty contain. As Márquez pulls out the stops for the return of Bayardo with his bag of unopened letters we might think of this, with some ironic intent, as his letter aria. In *Cholera*, by contrast, the whole work is made generically and consciously of a piece with its affirmation of romance. In a larger way, the whole literary movement of which Márquez is a part may be associated with the renewed, sophisticated appreciation of opera.

It is also no accident perhaps that the 'operatic' moment in *Chronicle* should have involved Angela's letters. For the letters which played a subordinate role in the earlier work have become a dominant motif, and narrative means, in the later one. Angela's letters were her means of expressing an emotional truth for which there was no other outlet. A comparable use of a letter occurs with the death of Dr Urbino's father, Dr Marco Aurelio Urbino. This imposing public figure is not really known even to his own family until they read his posthumous letter 'de amor febril' (p. 170) / 'of feverish love' (p. 116) written to them on his death bed. This letter shows his given name to be indeed an appropriate one yet 'nunca antes de esa carta se le había mostrado tal como era en cuerpo y alma, por pura y simple timidez' (pp. 170–1) / 'before this letter he had never revealed himself body and soul out of pure and simple shyness' (p. 117).

But the letters of Florentino are a central narrative device defining the emotional ambivalence, and the fictional bracketing, of the romantic experience. They are a way of balancing and interrelating the kinds of truth and falsehood in romance. His early letters, along with Fermina's subsequent rejection of him, suggest the dangers of delusion. Yet in the longer term the impulse of these letters is vindicated when he finds a newly realistic mode of expression. He has to learn that the bubble of romance bursts when its truth is too crudely counted on, or literalised. Fermina is then so struck by the wisdom of these later letters, that she decides to keep them as a series and to think of them as a book. If this is a hint towards the traditional device of the correspondence which becomes the book we are reading, then it is a reminder of the partial origin of modern realist fiction in the epistolary novel of the eighteenth century.

In the eighteenth century, this device was usually a way of exploring levels of sincerity in the character's self-presentation while keeping the whole form within that 'air of reality' which Henry James was to see as the hallmark of the novel tradition as he inherited it. There was a close homology between the narrative literalism of such fiction and the literalistic understanding of the ethics of sentiment in the same period.[12] If Márquez returns to some such value in the letter as mediating between the narrative form and the emotional ethic of the book, it is not by using the letters themselves as the narrative medium. The letters are always firmly placed within his own third-person narrative frame. Coming at the other end of the realist tradition, Márquez needs to use the letters not to reinforce the reality effect of his own narrative but to provide protective enclaves from such an effect. Only through that route does he then provide an implicit model for the ultimate meaning of his own story. Like both the opera and Florentino's letters, the novel creates a privileged but necessary space.

In sum, this novel vindicates its vision of romantic love through a constant, glancing texture of literary and cultural allusion. Yet the ultimately important emphasis has to be that, in keeping with Márquez' fundamental populism, these allusions never become too self-conscious, or detached from the narrative subject. The novel can be read innocently without being misread. The apparent casualness of the narrative is important, not just as a concealment of art: it is an aspect of the vision. The narrative bravura is part of the point. Henry James, D.H. Lawrence and Ivan Turgenev, while seeing the power of Flaubert, all saw something ultimately stultifying in the resolute imposition of his artistic will. For James and Turgenev particularly, we might say that the tragic vision of Flaubert was only indirectly revealed in his works and was most truly and fully embodied in the Sisyphean artistry these works imply. Flaubert himself was the true tragic hero of his oeuvre. By contrast, while showing a complete narrative mastery, Márquez creates the maximum open-endedness both of tone and of narrative resolution. The necessity and impossibility of romance are embodied in the teasing, flirtatious quality of the story-telling. Whereas the early fiction frequently had a sub-textual self-consciousness, this late work in particular puts its fictional play on the surface.

The critical danger, in seeking to make these effects explicit, is of breaking the butterfly upon a wheel. The glancingness is all. It may be helpful as a final emphasis, therefore, to give some examples of moments in which the playfully open-ended spirit of narrative self-consciousness in the work leaves the reader wondering how much to read into it at any given moment. The general spirit of the work creates a constant flicker of possibility, a kind of spray where the surface of its medium meets ours, such that one cannot be sure whether one has actually been splashed or has just imagined it. The meaning seems to lie more in the possibility than in the specific interpretation.

Are we, for example, to see a formal joke in the following incident which has little necessity from a purely narrative point of view?

> Alguna vez probo apenas una tisana de manzanilla, y la devolvió con una sola frase: 'Esta vaina sabe a ventana.' Tanto ella como las criadas se sorprendieron, porque nadie sabía de alguien que hubiera bebido una ventana hervida, pero cuando probaron la tisana tratando de entender, entendieron: sabía a ventana. (p. 324)

> Once he barely tasted some chamomile tea and returned it, with the single remark: 'This stuff tastes of window.' She and the servants were equally surprised because nobody had ever heard of anyone drinking boiled window, yet when they tried the tea in an effort to understand, they understood; it tasted of window. (pp. 226–7)

The reader here is in the same position as Fermina and the servants except that they can actually resolve the matter by tasting the tea. Fiction, like language itself, requires a consensual acceptance of external reality although fiction is also the pre-eminent medium through which the boundaries of consensus can be explored and renegotiated. At the level of language Dr Urbino's remark seems almost surrealist yet at the level of the fictional reality it turns out to have an accurately referential truth. Since we cannot taste the tea for ourselves, the remark retains for us its flickering ambiguity. It is strictly a play with the order of discourse itself, yet it is the more playful in being barely emergent from the order of the subject-matter. Behind the joke about the tea lies Dr Urbino's objection when food is not prepared with love. As was remarked in the preceding chapter, John Bayley would make this a fundamental principle of literary creation.

Or again, Florentino seems to incorporate a metafictional wit in the episode with the mirror. On one occasion during his fifty-year wait, he gets to see Fermina for several hours from fairly close up by the lucky placing of a mirror in a restaurant. He subsequently buys the mirror although its antique frame costs him dear. He is not interested in the frame but simply in the mirror which has contained the image of the beloved. Florentino is expressing his romantic extravagance by reversing the traditional image of realist vision. Once again, the episode is carried by its charm and can undoubtedly be read without such literary historical associations but part of its underlying toughness lies in its carrying the challenge into the enemy's territory. After all, even when used as a metaphor of realism, the image in the mirror is strictly a virtual one. The function of fiction at any time is not passive. It does not merely reflect but makes us reflect, and all reality is in some sense chosen.

The lightness of touch bears equally on the running comparison with Flaubert. Márquez is not necessarily placing *Cholera* on a footing with *Madame Bovary*. Indeed, the tact of the novel lies in its nice judgement of its own relative weight. Nor is it a question of displacing Flaubert's vision, as if proving it 'wrong'. Works of fictional imagination don't stand in that sort of relation to each other. It is rather a matter of taking a classic metaphysical vision, as incorporated in an equally classic formal mode, and using this to define a contrary one.

In fact, the danger here would be of allowing the order of allusion to take over too much so that the book becomes merely parasitical on an earlier one. There is a recognisable late twentieth-century fictional sub-genre of the rewritten classic. Jean Rhys's *Wide Sargasso Sea* (1966) is the most distinguished example, and *Flaubert's Parrot* a close runner-up. Márquez' allusiveness, however, steers well clear of this. His vision is there very much in its own right while using allusion, humorously and parenthetically, to define and place itself.

However, if this novel ends with his central characters challenging their social world and the very conditions of existence by their final, and as it were eternal, trip on the Magdalena river, this points towards the different world of Márquez' next novel, in which the weightiness of the historical subject could hardly be more ambitious.

NOTES

1. *El amor en el tiempos del colera* (Barcelona: Bruguera, 1985) p. 100; *Love in the Time of Cholera*, trans. Edith Grossman (London: Cape, 1988) p. 67.

2. Germaine Greer sees Márquez' whole treatment of the theme as 'ageist' although her reading seems humourlessly literalistic to me. See *The Change* (London: Hamish Hamilton, 1991) pp. 364–8.

3. See Denis de Rougemont, *Love in the Western World* (New York: Harper and Row, 1974); also trans. by Montgomery Belgion as *Passion and Society* (London: Faber, 1940).

4. For an extended discussion of this theme see Tony Tanner, *Adultery and the Novel* (Baltimore: Johns Hopkins University Press, 1979).

5. Letter to Alice James, Feb. 22, 1876. *Henry James: Letters*, ed. Leon Edel, Vol. II (London: Macmillan, 1975) pp. 29–30.

6. The published translation gives 'My heart...' but it is clear that Florentino is making a general, aphoristic reflection.

7. Stendhal, *Scarlet and Black*, trans. Margaret R. B. Shaw (Harmondsworth: Penguin, 1953) p. 149.

8. See the interview with Márquez, 'Of Love and Levitation', *TLS*, 20–26 October 1989, pp. 1151–65.

9. See *On Love*, trans. P. Sidney Woolf and C. N. Sidney Woolf (London: Duckworth, 1915). See especially chapter I, sections VI and XII.

10. In a lecture 'García Márquez and the Modernist Tradition' given at a conference on 'Gabriel García Márquez', Birkbeck College, London on 30 September 1988. The interest in popular music of the coastal region is a recurrent feature of Márquez' early journalism. See also Márquez' comment on *Hundred Years* when first working on it: 'It's like a bolero', *Fragrance*, p. 71.

11. 'Pierre Menard, Author of the Quixote', *Labyrinths*, pp. 62–71.

12. I have discussed the relationship of sentimentalist ethics and fictional form in *The Sentiment of Reality* (London: Unwin, 1983).

DAVID BUEHRER

"*A Second Chance on Earth*": *The Postmodern and the Post-apocalyptic in García Márquez's* Love in the Time of Cholera

On a day like today, my master William Faulkner said in this very place, "I refuse to admit the end of mankind." I should not feel myself worthy of standing where he once stood were I not fully conscious that, for the first time in the history of humanity, the colossal disaster which he refused to recognize thirty-two years ago is now simply a scientific possibility. Face to face with a reality that overwhelms us, one which over man's perceptions of time must have seemed a utopia, tellers of tales who, like me, are capable of believing anything, feel entitled to believe that it is not yet too late to undertake the notion of a minor utopia: a new and limitless utopia for life wherein no one can decide for others how they are to die, where love really can be true and happiness possible, where the lineal generations of one hundred years of solitude will have at last and for ever a second chance on earth.

Gabriel García Márquez,
Nobel Address, 1982.
Trans. Richard Cardwell

In John Barth's seminal 1980 essay on postmodernist fiction, "The Literature of Replenishment," he singles out Gabriel García Márquez and his novel *One Hundred Years of Solitude* as quintessential examples of the postmodern genre. For Barth, what distinguishes García Márquez's fiction is its "synthesis of straightforwardness and artifice, realism and magic and

From Critique 32, no. 1 (Fall 1990). © 1990 Helen Dwight Reid Educational Foundation myth, political passion and nonpolitical artistry, characterization and caricature, [and] humor and terror" (71)—all elements that characterize him as "an exemplary postmodernist and a master of the storyteller's art" (71). Yet prior to the publication of *Love in the Time of Cholera*, García Márquez stated in an interview that his forthcoming book would deal with the rather traditional themes of the "consciousness" of "old age, love and death" (qtd. in Simons 18). An obvious aesthetic contradiction seems to present itself here: how can a writer of contemporary fiction be perceived as an innovative postmodernist and a traditional storyteller at the same time? A provisional placement of García Márquez and his fiction into the broad social and cultural contexts of literary postmodernism also opens numerous critical trapdoors because a number of recent commentators, ranging from David Lodge to Gerald Graff,[1] have attempted to define this contemporary "school" in terms of its specific characteristics. However, many of these defined traits—fictional self-reflexiveness, ironic commentary, fragmentation of the individual character, and various manifestations of literary recombination, recycling, and repetition of forms and genres—may seem more typical to that handful of North American postmodernists (Barth, Barthelme, and Pynchon are the usual designates) who have received a plethora of critical attention. In García Márquez's *Love in the Time of Cholera*, this brand of literary postmodernism exists, but within the context of more traditionally expressed themes.

One such traditional theme that pervades the novel and serves to counter what theorists such as Gerald Graff and Todd Gitlin see as the inevitablist and fatalistic tendencies of much postmodern fiction[2] is a certain counter-strain of "left-over" humanism that García Márquez employs. That is, if the climate of a postmodern culture encourages a kind of "cultural anesthesia" and the fictional chronicling of contemporary anxieties of "aftermath, privatization, [and] weightlessness" (Gitlin 36), García Márquez's new novel seems vehement in dismissing such options of literary escapism. Instead, he chooses to look beyond the apocalyptic impetuses of a "numb, recombinant" (Gitlin 36) postmodern fiction and to present a novel refreshingly traditional (or, one might say, *post*-apocalyptic) in its assumption that "old age, love and death" as human virtues *can* survive the "blast" (here, the metaphor for apocalypse being the cholera epidemic), that subsurface feeling *can* incubate in and be unearthed from the fallout ashes, that the resources for self-renewal, contrary to the inevitablist theories, *are* possible. To all of these assumptions the fifty-year, nine-month, and four-day love affair of Florentino Ariza and Fermina Daza surely attests. *Love in the Time of Cholera* thus becomes García Márquez's answer to the seemingly apocalyptic ending of his *One Hundred Years of Solitude*: now, some twenty years later, humanity is endowed with the respite of "at last and for ever a second chance on earth," and what to the postmodern theorists may seem an inevitable despair becomes to the fictional creator of the "world" of the novel a humanistic finality and hope.

The humanistic question that *Love* addresses, however, seems crucial to the future of contemporary fiction, postmodern or otherwise: if "the end is near" or has already enveloped us, is it possible for a "new and saving *post-fiction*" (Bradbury 17) to emerge, one capable of retaining a "whole" depiction of the individual and of rescuing art from its presently corrupted status, "hip deep in debris" (Gitlin 35)? With this question in mind, a possibly misguided effort of attempting to pigeonhole García Márquez and *Love in the Time of Cholera* into one or another critical camp—modernism, postmodernism, magical realism, or others—may be valuable only inasmuch as it helps illuminate the novel as the product of a progressively humanistic contemporary sensibility. By the standards of Gitlin's above-cited argument, García Márquez would have to be grounded in something closer to a modern, and not postmodern, literary tradition because it would seem to be the modernist belief that art serves as *some* kind of "declaration of faith"—in God, in philosophy, or at least in the defined aesthetic of the work itself. As Raymond Leslie Williams sees it, García Márquez and other Latin American "boom" writers of the past two decades clearly follow a modernist "shaping" aesthetic of employing literary techniques "to seek order and express the ineffable in a world lacking order and waiting to be named" (7). The problem with this analysis, as Williams readily admits, is that García Márquez is not "consistently" modern—that is, in much of his fiction he at times seems to "cross-over" to a postmodern mode of writing that "subverts rather than seeks order, and has language as its primary subject" (Williams 8–9). Certainly the "language-as-subject" definition of postmodernism is valid for all of García Márquez's novels; and *Love*, with its lyricism and highly stylized embellishments, is no exception. But we should weigh this definition against more seemingly pessimistic analyses of postmodern fiction: if, as Gerald Graff claims, the postmodern mode represents a corrupt aesthetic based solely on "narcissism and artistic self-contempt" ("The Myth" 398) and has as its only objective the "conscious subversiveness of [the] literary past" ("The Myth" 403), is it possible to find an appropriate niche in such a hard-nosed "school" for the often blatantly humanistic García Márquez?

Love in the Time of Cholera may indeed qualify as and crosscover into postmodernism because of García Márquez's "living off borrowed materials" and his recycling of past cultural debris (Gitlin 36). In fact, Robert Fiddian's analysis of the novel finds García Márquez consciously parodying the nineteenth-century *folletín*,[3] hence producing a postmodern novel in which literary stereotypes are repudiated both in character and style and a lachrymose love story "masquerad[es] as a nineteenth-century work" (Fiddian 192). But such a reading assumes quite a bit—that García Márquez did set out systematically to burlesque a specific past literary genre, that Florentino Ariza and Fermina Daza were deliberately framed in comic-parodic terms, that García Márquez's language was purposely melodramatized and hence is reducible to a form of obvious farce that comments on a hackneyed former genre. Yet this seems overly reductionistic to the other extreme: the novel not as broad-minded humanism but merely as a postmodern ironic pastiche—a statement of anti-humanism—of such forms of ridiculous emotional high-mindedness. A modified approach between these extremes of literary branding—that is, the novel as modern declaration of faith or as postmodern "trashing" of faith—might be suggested by García Márquez's apparently fatalistic brand of humanism[4] as it surfaces in the novel, or by a faith in the renewal of human emotions that is partially tainted by the author's foreknowledge of death. Such a compromise positioning of *Love*—neither pure faith in the immutability of man nor outright debunking of his pretentious nature—may better serve its authorial intent and relieve it from an "either/or" status in terms of its "place" in the contemporary literary canon.

The novel is loosely "about" one of those conventions of the nineteenth-century *follétin*: the "love triangle," here of Dr. Juvenal Urbino, his wife, Fermina Daza, and Florentino Ariza, the love-sick poet who has waited "fifty years, nine months, and four days" to restate a pledge of "eternal fidelity and everlasting love" (50)[5] to Fermina, the now elderly sweetheart of his youth. Certainly the tone for a melodramatic, lachrymose portrayal of the trials of unrequited love is established (as Fiddian suggests), but perhaps García Márquez wants us to take him, and his seemingly stereotypical characters, more literally than we at first want to or believe we can (late twentieth-century wallowers in the "debris" and disillusionment of postmodern culture that we are). What are the implications, for instance, of a character like Florentino Ariza, a hopeless romantic who takes on the obstacles of both cultural restrictions and the finite nature of time—in this case, a half-century of *his* life—like a "stubborn warrior against age and death, and in the name of [eternal] love" (Pynchon 47) for a fickle teenage girl who long ago jilted him? To turn such a character into an absurd, parodic model of a past literary "type" would be the knee-jerk postmodernist response. After all, most insightful postmodern fiction writers have realized that literary "characters" are little more than "sentimental attachments [which have] decomposed" (see Gitlin 35) like the culture around them, or that such writers with their savage wit are helping to disassemble. Who in our contemporary cultural milieu would take seriously (or with a straight face) the description of a female "heroine" (even this word betrays a "sentimental" bias that has by now been overwhelmingly abandoned) like *Love*'s Fermina Daza, a "beautiful adolescent with ... almond shaped eyes" and with the "natural haughtiness ... [of] her doe's gait making her seem immune to gravity" (56)? Most characters of postmodern literature are *hardly* so defined, if they are defined at all.[6] Without any clear bearings within the massiveness of society, the postmodern character is not a quester after any individual definition of the self (as may be true for a modern character like Jay Gatsby) but instead exudes complacency and, like Barthelme's bored Snow White, embodies "the comic impossibility of heroism in a world paralyzed by self-consciousness" (Graff, "Babbitt" 326).

But taken seriously in a traditional sense as well as comically in a postmodern one, *Love*'s characters, specifically Florentino and Fermina, stand as ideal projections of the possibility of human emotionality, even within a drab postmodern society that stifles "the real news of subsurface feeling" (Gitlin 36). It is as if García Márquez has endowed his characters with enough traits of traditional humanistic belief to balance whatever postmodern features may be working to disassemble them.[7] Unlike his contemporary, Robbe-Grillet, who believes that the "death of character" is the necessary end result of a fiction that, like the culture that bore it, is morally defunct and socially fragmented, García Márquez feels that the resources for "self"-renewal *are* possible, that the human character and its fictional counterpart need not be sucked into the vacuum of a cultural entropy, that the "resurrection of the human body" (Pynchon 47) and a corresponding faith in human immutability, though at present fashionably scoffed at, *are* achieveable, albeit only in a created "minor utopia." Such a traditional humanistic faith is "revolutionary," as Pynchon puts it (47), because it stands in dogged resistance to the "cultural anesthesia" (Gitlin 36) that a postmodern society is supposed to foster. The audacity of a character's actually believing in a concept as ephemeral as "eternal love" (and surely Florentino does, though his life-long series of sexual liaisons somewhat lessen or make comic his sincerity)—a concept we all assumed long ago dead, or at least ripe presently for parodic debasement—in essence challenges the belief that a postmodern culture necessitates emotional dearth.

Similarly, the defined "wholeness" of García Márquez's characters, complete with broad-ranging human feelings and desires, suggests that he is not willing to "coast down the [postmodern] currents of least resistance" (Gitlin 36) as far as man's transformative power over himself and his present environment is concerned. Florentino's fifty-year wait for "everlasting love" seems to be the strongest metaphor for this authorial thrust: the depiction of a *post*-"cultural anesthesia" stage in which, after years of having to *refuse* to feel, the character converts his deprivation into an all-the-more acute, cathartic emotional response. Instead of taking us down those currents of least resistance like a good postmodernist should, García Márquez tosses the readers of *Love* upon the rapids of the "reborn" emotional response: we drift from an apocalyptic freeze or cauterization of emotions to the tropical heat or vitality of a finally consummated, long-incubating love affair. If Florentino and Fermina can be called "postmodern" characters, therefore, it is only in the role they play as embodiments of the "saving post-fiction" that García Márquez, much like Saul Bellow in his character-dominated, humanistic novels (Bradbury 17–19), seems determined to create. "Aftermath, privatization [and] weightlessness" (Gitlin 363 may be the milieu of our postmodern culture, but the *post*-state to the deprivation of feeling seems to be a more intense counter-response to the years of emotional subterfuge, a state tied intrinsically to García Márquez's "minor utopia" of history and setting that is his fictional world of the novel.

What is particular about the setting and history of *Love*, unlike its predecessor *One Hundred Years of Solitude*, is the sense in which "magical realism"[8] is no longer a necessary prerequisite to the making of the Garcíamarquezine novelistic environment. As Pynchon sees it in his review of the novel, the "reality" of love and the possibility of its ultimate extinction become *Love*'s "indispensable driving forces," whereas magic in all its guises and forms becomes peripheralized or "at least more thoughtfully deployed in the service of an expanded vision, matured, darker than before but no less clement" (49). This is not to say that *all* trace of "magic"—i.e., the plague of insomnia, the ascension of Remedios the Beauty in *One Hundred Years*—is missing in *Love*: there is something ultimately "unreal" and comic in the narrator's casual calculation of Florentino's 622 "long-term liaisons, apart from ... countless fleeting adventures" (152) during the romantic's life in seclusion from his "real" love, Fermina, for example. But this novel of "aftermath" presents more definably a sequel or follow-up stage to what Gerald Martin sees as García Márquez's switch to *social* (and, hence, traditional) reality as opposed to magical reality, a switch that occurs with the so-called "apocalyptic" ending of *One Hundred Years* (111). Certainly in *Love* García Márquez is "creating" his own fictional world in that ontological sense that Brian McHale sees as requisite to any postmodern novel (10),[9] yet in terms of the post-apocalyptic thesis suggested earlier, *Love* can be viewed as symbolic of a particular period of historical *de*-evolution in Latin America. In the setting of a small Colombian coastal town, a rough composite of Cartagena, the home of the author's parents, and Barranquilla, during the half-century of Florentino Ariza's incubating love, significant social and historical changes transpire in Latin America's perception of itself as a dream-land at last awakening to form a new reality from the fragments of cultural debris that remain. Here, then, the postmodern and the traditional are colliding on the same fictional plane: although the characters must employ so-called postmodern methods of recycling and recombination to revitalize their environment, they must do so in a less than magical world and through the power of their own human potentialities. In this sense, as Aureliano Babilinia's "deciphering" of the manuscripts of history at the close of *One Hundred Years* signals the end of historical era of neo-colonialism and the apocalyptic starting point for a people's new definition of themselves (Martin 112), so the finally consummated love of Florentino and Fermina in old age as the climax of *Love* signals the beginning of a "new era," a post-apocalyptic one that sees the return to traditional humanistic values as its wellspring of hope.

In this far-reaching cultural sense, therefore, it is possible to see why García Márquez chose the period 1880–1930 in which to shape his allegory of "aftermath and privatization" and the possibilities for cultural continuation that proceed it. The "environment" of *Love* concerns the antitheses of this volatile and changing history and the characters that embody it. There is Dr. Juvenal Urbino, figurehead for the "last" nineteenth-century hero, well-born, arrogant, but along with his venerable family showing signs of the decay of an old order—possibly the era of neo-colonialism itself—and its progressive deterioration into shabby genteelism. There is Florentino, who is born in poverty but rises to social prominence as a self-made man and president of the River Company at the precise period that one century turns over and collides with the nouveau riche next one. Finally, there is Fermina, another last of a dying breed, this time of youthful debutantes with shady family histories, who eventually throws personal pretension and social prominence to the wind by accepting the sexual but "everlasting" love of Florentino *even* in old age. Within this historical conflux looms that central symbol for one age threatening the obliteration of a former one: the "cholera" epidemic, the apocalyptic proliferation of death over a half-century, which, by the ambiguity of García Márquez's native Spanish, can be perceived as either the fatal disease itself—*el colera*—or as the general condition of choler, anger, and finally warfare—*la colera*—that in its more sweeping sense signifies "a devastating force, a plague, whose only meaning is death on a massive scale" (Pynchon 47). For those who survive it as well as those who fight it (Urbino through medicine, Florentino through faith in erotic love), it is the world-ending plague of the era, out of which either the culture will persevere amidst increasing increments of decay or will succumb to eventual, unalterable disintegration. Such a period of microcosmic apocalypse thus becomes the atemporal setting of García Márquez's "historiographic metafiction" (Hutcheon 285)—a fiction that comments not only upon the social conditions that can or cannot make self-renewal possible, but that also accepts the integral role the creation of the fictional world plays in "surviving" (albeit in an only "minor utopia") the effects of the apocalyptic "fallout." The symbol of the phoenix, though grossly overused to the point of cliché, nevertheless seems most applicable to the general tenor of the question inherent in García Márquez's narrative: after decimation—environmental, cultural, social, even personal—what can possibly remain to revive a world spent by abuse and its own historical exhaustion?

Fiddian reduces the answer to such a question to "heterosexual love" (197), but in a broader sense what survives is a more general "love among the ruins"—that is, the indomitable quality of human emotion in the face of historical and cultural forces bent on forcing its demise. It thus becomes a question of whether the extinction of a "world"—by a physical as well as what might be termed a modern socioeconomic "plague"—necessitates the extinction of that world's underlying "dominant," which, in García Márquez's humanistic ideology, is *human* love, in *all* its manifestations. This then is how and where the trans-generational milieu of *Love* takes on its postmodern "maker's" formation and "recombination of hand-me-down scraps" (Gitlin 35)—those remains or ashes of historical apocalypse, no matter its specific form—into a "new" world, or the resurrection of a "new Eden." The "blast" may have devastated the environment, but paradoxically, it has served only to purify the emotions that have endured. This ontological perspective of a "new world" salvaged from the shards of an old one is beautifully displayed in the description of the turn-of-the-century balloon trip taken by Fermina and her husband:

> From the sky they could see, just as God saw them, the ruins of the very old and heroic city of Cartagena de Indias, the most beautiful in the world, abandoned by its inhabitants because of the sieges of the English and the atrocities of the buccaneers. They saw the walls, still intact, the brambles in the streets, the fortifications devoured by heartsease, the marble palaces and the golden altars and the viceroys rotting with plague inside their armour. (226)

Fermina and Florentino later are to become the unchosen proprietors of this new world of *post* or *after*-history, therefore—*after* neo-colonialism, *after* the "progress" of industrialization (that is supposed to bring with it "order" and "moral clarity," yet such virtues, in a postmodern culture, have progressively disintegrated [Gitlin 36]), but before what?

García Márquez firmly embeds his new "heroes" in the "aftermath" of history that is the twentieth-century, but he is not so idealistic as to confess that "love conquers all" and in *all* situations, because his humanism is one tempered by the realities of human existence in a corrupt, decrepit age. For instance, while professing his state of "virginity" to the aged Fermina (339), Florentino's idealization of love is blemished by our knowledge not only of his lifetime of countless sexual trysts, but especially of that one that concludes with the suicide of his 14-year-old charge, América Vicuña (336). This, then, seems to be García Márquez's mature brand of humanism at work: the "new Eden" that his old lovers resurrect from the ashes (or the dry riverbed) will not be a purely Pollyannaic one—Florentino's profession to Fermina of his spotless nature is farcical—but one tempered by the cold reality of imminent human death (América Vicuña's is a mere foreknowledge of the lovers' own). It is as if García Márquez's faith in and hope for a "minor utopia" and "second chance on earth," however liberating, must always remain clouded by the ominous threat of self-destruction: after all, if the earth itself (evidenced at the novel's close by the setting of deforestation on the Magdalena River) can be permanently destroyed, what is to stop human emotionality, with the death of the body, from succumbing possibly to a similar fate?

It is the river, finally, the Great Magdalena (in Spanish, the "river of life") on which Florentino Ariza had made his livelihood but left one day on a journey of forgetting only to return, regardless of the cost, to wait for the day that the widowed Fermina Daza would be his, that García Márquez uses at the close of *Love* to consolidate his vision of humanistic hope amidst the fallout of historical apocalypse. As they board the *New Fidelity* (a name loaded with the weight of the lovers' re-established vow to each other) for what will be a journey without end, Florentino and Fermina at once evidence the signs that a half-century of apocalyptic waste has wrecked on a formerly Edenic setting:

> ... the Magdalena, father of waters, one of the great rivers of the world, was only an illusion of memory. ... Fifty years of uncontrolled deforestation had destroyed the river: the boilers of the riverboats had consumed the thick forest of colossal trees. ... The hunters for skins ... had exterminated the alligators that, with yawning mouths, had played dead for hours on end in the gullies along the shore as they lay in wait for the butterflies, the parrots with their shrieking and the monkeys with their lunatic screams

had died out as the foliage was destroyed, the manatees with their
great breasts that had nursed their young and wept on the banks
in a for woman's voice were an extinct species, annihilated. (331)

Confronted by this ecological wasteland, partly of their own making (after
all, Florentino's ships have "consumed" much of the lumber), by "the
nauseating stench of corpses floating down to the sea" and the "vast silence
of the ravaged land" (336), the lovers and their at-last-sanctioned desire seem
to have arrived too late. They now find themselves the sole inheritors of a
world raped beyond recognition, where vague emotional longings like "love"
and "fidelity" have little right or place to exist. This is the world-stage of *post-*
apocalypse that García Márquez last left us with at the end of *One Hundred
Years of Solitude*, as Aureliano Babilonia, deciphering the cryptic manuscripts,
discovers at the same moment the cold realization that his "history" is over,
the Buendía house ravaged by the cyclone of dogged time, his own and his
family's lineal heritage of "one hundred years of solitude" left in the
devastated state of never being endowed "a second opportunity on earth"
(383). Hence, the time (or reality) after such apocalypse can no longer be
conceived of as "magical." In *Love*, it is the time and setting of the "other"
America, scarred by its own complacency and the exploitation of others, but
it is also a time beyond time, beyond apocalypse, and therefore a mythical
past that García Márquez must conceive (as his Nobel address surely
suggests) as a projected, possible future. But if physically drained and
exhausted by the forces of its own history, a *post*modern "heart of darkness"
from which there seems no return, the river of *Love* is also, paradoxically, the
depthless reservoir that symbolizes the rebirth of human emotions. "By the
time he [Florentino] realized the truth, there was nothing anyone could do
except bring in a new river" (337). If this environmental option seems
practicably impossible, García Márquez *does* seem to be admitting that a
"new river" or source of emotional renewal is possible—one that is conceived
or created by immutable *human* potentialities. Just as modern man's reckless
"progress" is capable of ecological destruction, his *post*modern successor—
blindly, naively, but yet necessarily—must remain (or *survive*) to reconstruct
from the debris a vestige of human faith and hope. Here, then, is postmodern
man serving a decidedly *positive* function: instead of drifting ignorantly down
those "currents of least resistance" that Gitlin perceives as our self-evident
fate both in art *and* life, Florentino and Fermina confront, at a time when
they should know better (as Fermina's daughter smugly implies), the
turbulent waters of life head on, overwhelmed finally, like the captain of the
New Fidelity, "by the belated suspicion that it is life, more than death, that has
no limits" (348).

The force of ontological, world-creating "suspicion" alone, however, does not make them the postmodern characters of a postmodern author. In the vague but significant sense that both characters and García Márquez himself recognize that they are left with only the cultural debris or fragments of a world (real or fictional) to reconstruct, they are postmodern. But García Márquez is hardly content to wallow and eventually drown in such suffocating debris: face-to-face with the "reality" that is nothing less than the "scientific possibility" of the end of the world, a human writer admits (and prays for) "at last and forever" the second chance for man on earth that Florentino and Fermina are granted in their old age. Such traditional faith in human immutability could quite easily be perceived, especially in our postmodern culture, as naive utopianism that human reality every day persistently contradicts. But if a passive hopelessness in feeling historically stranded is the typical postmodernist's response, García Márquez and the fictional characters who speak eloquently for him cannot accept such trendy resignation: whether it is specifically that "other" America, his Latin America that has just awakened from its nightmare of twentieth-century history, or whether through this sleepy, tropical setting he is evoking a universal condition, García Márquez in *Love in the Time of Cholera* is willing to take the daring "leap of faith" on the side of *man himself* over the inevitablist theories or possibilities man can create for himself. In taking such a seemingly unpopular but obviously essential stand, García Márquez is responsible in the process for creating that brand of "new and saving post-fiction" that has as its subject "not ... the death of the self or the collapse of the referential" (Bradbury 18), but a character of broad humanistic vision who is capable still of "love," the most elusive of all emotional abstractions, in a world of past and ever-impending "cholera"—plague, war, apocalypse. Although "forever" (348) is a long time to believe man can survive, especially in an atomic age, García Márquez would have nothing less for Florentino and Fermina, for nothing but that love he bestows to them is capable of that rejuvenating power of hope that he sees as paramount to our survival as a race.

NOTES

1. Lodge, in his essay "Postmodernist Fiction" (in *The Modes of Modern Writing: Metaphor, Metonymy, and the Typology of Modern Literature*. Ithaca: Cornell UP, 1977: 220–245), for instance, includes as his "list" of postmodern categories "Contradiction," "Permutation," "Discontinuity," "Randomness," "Excess," and the "Short-Circuit," with corresponding examples (mainly from American fiction) of each. See Graff's seminal essays "The Myth of the Postmodernist Breakthrough" and "Babbitt at the Abyss" (both listed in Works Cited) for his varying "lists" of postmodern characteristics.

2. In "The Myth of the Postmodernist Breakthrough" Graff, for instance, defines the postmodern as serving the essentially "apocalyptic" function of revealing the

destructiveness and uselessness of contemporary art and reality (392). Gitlin's dark analysis of postmodern culture and its productions, in "Hip-Deep in Post-modernism," continues Graff's apocalyptic thesis: postmodernism (and especially its literary representations) is merely a form of "anticipatory shell-shock" (36), as if "the bomb" has already fallen. Hence, although postmodern fiction must necessarily invoke the recycling of past cultural debris, it tends to leave its reader feeling "historically stranded—after the 1960s, but before what?" (Gitlin 36). In fact, at the close of his article Gitlin seems to be pleading for a kind of contemporary fiction that does not merely "coast down the currents of least resistance" (36), as a postmodern culture might heartily encourage. Perhaps the return to traditionalism in what might be termed a *post*-apocalyptic fiction—García Márquez's *Love*—is what Gitlin is desiring.

3. The *folletín* was that brand of sentimental romance novel best characterized in Latin America by Jorge Isaac's *María*.

4. Fiddian as well cites Fermina's obsession with a newspaper report, as she travels with Florentino on the *New Fidelity*, concerning the brutal murder of an elderly couple on a similar riverboat as they depart on a second honeymoon (Love 460–61) as evidence of García Márquez's own "intimation of mortality" (199–200) and thus nuance-ridden "humanism."

5. All page references are to Gabriel García Márquez's *Love in the Time of Cholera*, trans. Edith Grossman, New York: Knopf, 1988 (except where otherwise indicated).

6. In "Babbitt at the Abyss," for instance, Graff sees the only distinguishable trait of a postmodern character to be his "amiable passivity" and apathy in the face of a constantly changing contemporary society, leading to a "diffuse, unfocused, protean self which cannot define issues in any determinate way" (309).

7. García Márquez, in fact, seems to be answering with his characters Malcolm Bradbury's complaint that the contemporary novel's depiction of "the complexity of the individual was never more necessary, since in our time so many processes and so many theories are arrayed against it" (see his Introduction to *Saul Bellow* 18).

8. John Brushwood in a recent article succinctly defined this term as the "boom" fictional category in which the marvelous "exists naturally; one does not have to invent strange juxtapositions/associations" (see his "Two Views of the Boom: North and South," *Latin American Literary Review* 15.29 [January–June 1987]: 19–20). For further definitions of "magical realism" and a brief summary of its history as a movement, see Angel Flores's "Magical Realism in Spanish American Fiction" (*Hispania* 38 [May 1955]: 187–192).

9. McGrath, in the opening chapter of his study *Postmodernist Fiction* (1987), uses the Russian formalist concept of the "dominant" to distinguish modernist from postmodernist novels. By his analysis, the essential difference (i.e., common denominator, or "dominant") between the modern and the postmodern text involves the latter's shifting of the underlying dominant from problems of knowing to problems of "modes of being—from an epistemological dominant to an ontological one" (10). For the postmodern novelist (and McGrath includes García Márquez under this rank), therefore, ontology, or "a theoretical description of a universe" (27)—not the universe, but any universe, real or created—becomes his overriding concern, and his text thus emphasizes questions such as "Which world is this? What is to be done with it? ... What is a world? What kinds of worlds are there ... [and] what happens when different kinds of worlds are placed in confrontation? ... How is a projected world structured?" (10).

WORKS CITED

Barth, John. "The Literature of Replenishment: Postmodernist Fiction." *The Atlantic January* 1980: 65–71.

Bradbury, Malcolm. Introduction: "Saul Bellow and the Contemporary Novel." *Saul Bellow*. London, New York: Methuen, 1982. 15–34.

Fiddian, Robin. "A Prospective Post-Script: Apropos of *Love in the Time of Cholera*." *Gabriel García Márquez: New Readings*. Eds. Bernard McGuirk and Richard Cardwell. New York and London: Cambridge UP, 1987. 191–205.

García Márquez, Gabriel. *Love in the Time of Cholera*. Trans. Edith Grossman. New York: Knopf, 1988.

———. *One Hundred Years of Solitude*. Trans. Gregory Rabassa. New York: Harper, 1970.

———. "The Solitude of Latin America: Nobel Address 1982." Trans. Richard Cardwell. New York and London: Cambridge UP, 1987. 207–211.

Gitlin, Todd. "Hip-Deep in Post-modernism." *New York Times Book Review* 6 November 1988: 1, 35–36.

Graff, Gerald. "Babbitt at the Abyss: The Social Context of Postmodern American Fiction." *TriQuarterly* 33 (1975): 305–337.

———. "The Myth of the Postmodernist Breakthrough," *TriQuarterly* 26 (Winter 1973): 383–417.

Hutcheon, Linda. "'The Pastime of Past Time': Fiction, History, Historiographic Metafiction." *Genre* 20 (Fall/Winter 1987): 285–305.

Martin, Gerald. "On 'Magical' and Social Realism in García Márquez." *Gabriel García Márquez: New Readings*. Eds. Bernard McGuirk and Richard Cardwell. New York and London: Cambridge UP, 1987. 95–116.

McHale, Brian. "From Modernist to Postmodernist Fiction: Change of Dominant." *Postmodernist Fiction*. New York: Methuen, 1987. 3–25.

Pynchon, Thomas. "The Heart's Eternal Vow." Review of *Love in the Time of Cholera*. *New York Times Book Review* 10 April 1988: 1, 47, 49.

Simons, Marlise. "Love and Age: A Talk With García Márquez." *New York Times Book Review* I April 1985: 1, 18–19.

Williams, Raymond Leslie. "Preface" to *Special Issue: The Boom in Retrospect*. *Latin American Literary Review* 15.29 (January–June 1987): 7–11.

MABEL MORAÑA

Modernity and Marginality in
Love in the Time of Cholera

The brilliant and complex prose of Gabriel García Márquez has still not been sufficiently analyzed for its ideological implications. His "paper human beings" (to use Roland Barthes's term for literature's men and women) both evokes and surpasses other prototypical literary representations as well as the actual protagonists of Latin American history. His patriarchs and matriarchs, his colonels, the lyricism and solitude of his lonely characters, his legendary and magical families, tenuously evoke known reality. At the same time, it is obvious that they are not susceptible to a literal reading. They victoriously transcend mere referentiality and at times appear to be figments of poetic license.

Criticism has generally identified the Latin American question in his work with certain elements related to basic political and economic problems. In this case, critics frequently limit themselves to demonstrating explicit references to a particular period which then would seem simply to lend authority to the documentary basis that supports the second term of the well-known formula, "magic realism." It is true that the discourse of transnational capitalism, the themes of civil war, of power, the failure of institutions, repression, and popular resistance constantly surface in García Márquez' texts, but they constitute more a background, an inevitable referential framework that is nevertheless mediated by the excesses of fantasy. Even "la

From *Studies in Twentieth Century Literature* 14, no. 1 (Winter 1990). © 1990 *Studies in Twentieth Century Literature*.

violencia," the period of violence in Colombia in the forties and fifties, is absorbed into his stories much in the way that the Mexican Revolution is absorbed into the stories of Juan Rulfo. This is compatible with the statements that García Márquez has made on more than one occasion—that he wishes to focus on the repercussions of violence rather than on its causes or its application.[1] In any case, attempts at ideological analysis have not yet tackled the structures underlying the narrative as a whole nor the deployment of this ideological structure within contemporary Latin America.[2]

The world of García Márquez is both familiar and remote to the reader. It is influenced on the one hand by the Cuban Revolution and yet at the same time, it is focussed on the turn of the century. On the one hand, García Márquez's narrative obeys the stylistic requirements of "high art," and yet it comes under the diverse influences of popular culture. To literature, it restores its time-honored mission of entertaining by means of the mere act of narrating, suggesting that the texture in which the real and the imaginary, the autobiographical and the collective, are intermingled has no justification beyond the revival of the "forgotten art of telling stories."[3]

No other work illustrates this so completely as *Love in the Time of Cholera*, for what is instantly obvious in this novel is the manner in which the author reworks in an incredibly fresh style the clichés of romanticism or rather, as he himself acutely puts it, "the late romanticism of the Caribbean."[4] In fact the novel can be seen as a kind of frieze on which are displayed all possible stages of love—in youth and old age, Platonic and erotic, lawful and unlawful, ephemeral and eternal, childlike yet sublime.

The story details the "sentimental education" of Florentino Ariza, a prototype of the "mad hero," and his faithfulness to a youthful love which can be consummated only after half a century.[5] The linking of love and old age constitutes a distinct thematic emphasis of the narrative. What distinguishes the novel would thus appear to be the challenge of taking on a seemingly worn-out theme—one that has had such a significant role in Western culture especially in the nineteenth century, and the insertion of this theme into the "third age," which has been so poorly represented in literature. This "mise en abime" at the thematic level is counterbalanced by the deceptively simple plot and structure. Once again García Márquez's narrative seems to float off in a sumptuous exercise of virtuosity into the freedom of lyrical pleasure.[6] In this essay, I wish to offer a different reading of the Colombian writer's novel. I am, however, less interested in probing beneath the "surface structure" of the work than in exploring the scope of a narrative method that I hope will illuminate elements to be found in the rest of García Márquez's writing.

SYMMETRY AS A STRUCTURING PRINCIPLE

García Márquez has himself commented intuitively (but with some accuracy) on the symmetrical construction of *Love in the Time of Cholera*:

> The novel tends towards symmetry. It has an axis and as the axis moves towards the left or the right, the structure is reflected in the two parallel parts. [The structure], therefore, tends towards symmetry until it finds its center, though I do not know exactly where this lies—perhaps at the moment when Fermina who is already an old woman comes back from a journey, meets Florentino in a movie theater where he for the first time realizes that she is an old woman.[7]

On the temporal level, there is an obvious symmetry because the novel generally follows the structure of biography, but there are other forms of symmetry with wider implications.[8] The most obvious of these is the thematic symmetry provided by the love triangle of Fermina, her husband and Florentino. At various moments of their lives and in different ways, Fermina answers to the needs of both men and in great measure their lives are shaped by this response. Her "regulating function"[9] rests on her capacity to control the laws that rule the lives of the other two people to such an extent that García Márquez himself was able to summarize her narrative function thus: "she is the strong one, Fermina Daza. She is the novel."[10]

However this central role of the female character is no more than the anecdote that underlies a "deeper" symmetry. In effect, the novel juxtaposes beneath the thematic surface not only two different male characters with different world views, but also the tense coexistence of two social projects.

In *Love in the Time of Cholera*, García Márquez to some extent reworks the suspense novel. The conflict between the two projects is latent, for the author sacrifices the dramatic possibilities of conflict to a temporal development whose melancholy overtones are a sign of the times. The fin-de-siècle nostalgia sublimates violence and possible antagonisms by suggesting that there is a time and a place for everything and by means of a well-defined individualism which has the effect of a false consciousness. As Dr. Urbino remarks, "the century changes for everyone except for us," a class vision that is validated by the author himself.[11]

In any case, the text offers the reader two diverse articulations between the individual and the social reality of the historical period in the Caribbean cultural area which is the setting of the novel. Both are symmetrically arranged around the female character whose function as link and catalyst I will explain later on. The first of these articulations corresponds to the project of modernization and is actualized in Dr. Urbino, a professional man of refined tastes educated in Europe who enjoys great social prestige. The second articulation is that represented by Florentino Ariza, the exaggerated *criollo* romantic who is actualized in the novel through progressively more archaic models.[12] Non-productive, a dilettante, self-centered, Florentino incarnates the values of the past, which he perpetuates and projects with moving persistence. His status as a "problematic hero" consists precisely in that persistence of romantic attitudes in an era of change and in his marginality with respect to manners and characters through whom the social order and dominant values are expressed. Both projects coexist in the "time of cholera," an expression that refers to a period of natural violence when progress had not yet managed to control social evils (city sanitation, political turbulence) or natural evils (sickness). Because of this conventional link between love and illness, the novel again conceals its basic problematic.[13]

The theme of love allows the representation and the confrontation of two different cultural orders which are revealed through taste, values, language, and attitudes. Along with the theme of old age, this adds a temporal element that not only carries the representational possibilities to the extreme but also converts conflicts into processes and stages into cycles.

The exploration of love takes place both on a vertical and a horizontal plane. The vertical aspect consists of a detailed demonstration and in-depth exploration. The horizontal aspect unfolds the evolution of the affair. The exploration of both horizontal and vertical axes corresponds to the "problematic hero," Florentino Ariza, who is committed to no project other than himself. At the same time, both masculine heroes are ideological representations. Each one incarnates a social project expressed through different symbols. For Dr. Urbino, cholera demonstrates the vulnerability of a social order that he struggles to ameliorate and that demands progress and modernization. The cholera epidemic is the objective proof both of his limitations and his need for a Utopian project. For Florentino, navigation symbolizes his marginalization. His constant passage across the boundaries of a social system into which he is never integrated, which he crosses or passes through without ever staying in one place, provides a continuous and intuitive life apprenticeship. Secondly and significantly, there is his writing which is a mode of expression, of persuasion or pretense and which provides the strategies by means of which he seeks access to the system, while displaying romantic faith in the word."[14]

The class origins of both characters, the social and private spaces in which they move, their ways of living over a period of time, their pleasures, their relationship to convention, their place within the workforce, their connections with the community all indicate the varied levels on which separately and symmetrically they are articulated with the social system. Both come together in relation to a woman whose character deliberately represents upward social mobility into a higher class and the consolidation of a social position through marriage. Fermina acts both as nexus between the two male characters and as a stabilizing mechanism because of her ability to operate in both registers and to use time in her favor. The ideological structuring of the novel and its reconstruction of the fin de siècle aesthetic apparatus thus correspond to this two-fold scheme by which the social division that heralded the new century is revealed.

MODERNIZATION

In his important book, *The Poverty of Progress*, E. Bradford Burns calls attention to the importance of modernizing projects as well as to "the ideology of progress" as catalysts in a devastating cultural struggle that took place in Latin America during the second half of the nineteenth century. The elite, spurred by the desire to emulate the developed countries, encouraged projects of urbanization and industrialization which were opposed to national reality, to tradition and to the needs of most of the population. This created a dramatic split between the potential wealth of the continent and the people's daily lives. As Burns indicates, progress and modernization were the words most commonly used in the political vocabulary of the period:

> Both words, used interchangeably hereafter, implied an admiration for the latest ideas, modes, values, inventions, and styles of Europe and the United States and a desire to adopt— rarely to adapt—them. The elites believed that "to progress" meant to recreate their nations as closely as possible to their European and North American models. They felt they would benefit from such a recreation, and by extension they assumed that their nations would benefit as well. They always identified (and confused) class well-being with national welfare.[15]

Nevertheless, as a consequence of the tension produced by the conflict between the modernization project and the alternatives that manifested themselves at the popular level, "violence emerged as a leitmotif the nineteenth century. ..."[16]

The period of technological change, political violence and uneven development of different social classes is well represented in *Love in the Time of Cholera* in the role of the elites in putting into effect a European model which was firmly underpinned by the ideology of positivism. Dr. Juvenal Urbino functions within the novel as the flagbearer of ideas and values associated with modernization. Educated in Paris, involved in public works, he is a rational man who at the same time loves the arts; he functions in the novel as the prototype of that sector of the privileged class that accepts the ideology of "order and progress" that it considers to be above sectarian party politics:

> Although he had always been considered a Liberal and had been in the habit of voting for that party's candidates, it was more a question of tradition than conviction, and he was perhaps the last member of the great families who still knelt in the street when the Archbishop's carriage drove by. He defined himself as a natural pacifist, a partisan of definitive reconciliation between Liberals and Conservatives for the good of the nation. But his public conduct was so autonomous that no group claimed him for its own: the Liberals considered him a Gothic troglodyte, the Conservatives said he was almost a Mason, and the Masons repudiated him as a secret cleric in the service of the Holy See. His less savage critics thought he was just an aristocrat enraptured by the delights of the Poetic Festival while the nation bled to death in an endless civil war. (44)

His expeditions to Paris (from which he returns steeped in rationalism and dazzled by the latest technological inventions) reaffirm his Messianic role with respect to the dispossessed classes—a role that corresponds to the enlightened paternalism of the elites of the period.

The cholera epidemic brings him, as a guardian of social health, into contact with his social milieu. His incursions into the marginal are rapid and infrequent, but they serve to corroborate his values and his belief that "the city, his city, stood unchanging on the edge of time: the same burning dry city of his nocturnal terrors and the solitary pleasures of puberty, where flowers rusted and salt corroded, where nothing had happened for four centuries except a slow aging among withered laurels and putrefying swamps" (16).

The promiscuous vitality of the slave quarters, that "death-trap of the poor," which Juvenal Urbino visits at the beginning of the novel, contrasts with the "European coherence" of his mansion furnished with Turkish carpets, Sèvres porcelain, and boasting a music room and a splendid library in which a parrot sings French as a sign of the symbiosis of Europeanization and Caribbean culture.

Around the figure of Juvenal Urbino the author weaves a socioeconomic network that is the index of modernity. The inauguration of air mail, balloon rides, the progress of navigation, of ground transport and the media, register the practical effects of fin-de-siècle modernization. The ideas of progress and development were conflated, so that progress was generally measured against external factors or by means of quantitative indices that did not take into account with any precision the privileging of certain social sectors because of development and the relation between these sectors and the potential wealth of the nation.[17]

Modernization presupposes social order, but nevertheless it coexists with violence. Cholera, violence and modernization form a representational triad that is early perceived in the novel. Thus, for example, at the beginning of the fifth section, when Dr. Urbino and his wife make their first trip in a balloon for the celebration of the new century, they observe through a telescope the banana plantations and discover a number of dead bodies which they attribute to the cholera epidemic.

"Well, it must be a very special form of cholera," [Urbino] said, "because every single corpse has received the coup de grace through the back of the neck" (117).

The ideas of reason, progress, social prestige and integration and public duty come together in the character of Juvenal Urbino and the social sector he represents; his social origin and vital experience stand in physical and psychological contrast to Florentino Ariza, who serves as a kind of anti-model.

MARGINALITY

Florentino Ariza represents not so much a coherent and conscious alternative to modernization as, on the one hand, a vitality that escapes the control of instrumental reason and, on the other hand, a neo-romanticism that marks the persistence of tradition. As a synthesis of both these aspects, he actualizes the values of national culture as against European-style modernization which imposes its model of progress without respecting national identity.

In a social medium dominated by the ideology of progress, elite supremacy, and technological change, his character develops as an implied challenge to these hegemonic values. Florentino moves in marginal spaces (the lower-class neighborhoods of the city and brothels): he is a bastard and his vulnerable and somber appearance symbolizes his social condition. In describing him, the author invokes a racial aspect that reinforces the marginality that he shares with broad sectors of Latin America which are thrust towards the periphery of the system along with the "poor mulattos" who inhabit the city slums. In contrast to the dashing and worthy image of Dr. Urbino, Florentino Ariza was "bony and erect, his skin dark and clean-shaven, his eyes avid behind round spectacles in silver frames" (44).

The motif of the journey (which implies change and displacement, whether of a positive or negative nature) is constantly associated in the novel with his character and function. Yet, he only makes two journeys, the first after Fermina's wedding, when he is "raped" and thus arrives at the conclusion that "his illusory love for Fermina Daza could be replaced by an earthly passion" (p. 143). The second journey takes place at the end of the novel when he sails with Fermina Daza. However, his job with the shipping company constantly associates him with movement, an association that is also suggested (though more symbolically) by the promiscuity of his love life, which is a process of constant displacement from one woman to another, a kind of pilgrimage in which he goes through all the variations of sexuality and all of its transgressions. In his case, travel does not signify cultural and rational enlightenment as it does for Urbino on his expeditions to Europe, nor does it signify an escape as it does in the case of Fermina Daza's "journey of forgetting." For Florentino, the journey is the affirmation—and towards the end of the novel the perpetuation—of marginality.

Like the succession of casual affairs that make up his life and which coexist with his love for Fermina, transition implies for him the centrifugal move to a space on the periphery which, however, is always governed by its center. Florentino moves in the underworld of clandestine love affairs that provoke social censorship while at the same time he simultaneously conducts a constant courtship of Fermina, who, along with the aura and the values that surround her, is transformed into the permanent object of his desire. Florentino's ambition is to overcome his anonymity, and to gain access (however minimally) into the social system governed by principles and norms that are alien to his class and that systematically exclude him. His very constitutive articulation of love and old age situates him on a vital frontier which is beyond the limits established by a society whose governing principle is productivity (associated with the values of youth and social integration). Love at the age when Florentino and Fermina consummate theirs is "revolting" (323), a comment that speaks eloquently of the rigidity of the dominant conventions. The final journey up and down the river concentrates the motifs of love, old age, boat-travel, plague, marginality, social rejection and political violence, in a *summa* that is prolonged endlessly: "Forever" (348).

But love, in any form, is always somewhat marginal, for it is a rebellion against the conventions and values of a society entering rapidly into modernization. Its secrecy acts as a stimulus; obstacles make it more intense; even promiscuity makes it flower with extraordinary vital energy. It is alternatively "cataclysm," "lightning," "a deathly fall." It implies voracity, excess, and its symptoms are similar to those of "the disaster of cholera." Even Fermina associates "pleasure with secrecy" (128) and devotes herself to "solitary love," which awakens pangs of conscience (153–54). Only the domesticity that comes with marriage sets bounds to all the excesses of instinct and feeling, transforming love into something that might "almost be love" (205)—which is certainly not true of Florentino Ariza. In his case his singularity and his marginality are a way of life and a style that he cultivates by appropriating all the apparatus of romanticism as a parodic reconstruction which combines the romantic fin-de-siècle novel and women's popular romances. Here he is on the eve of the journey that will separate him temporarily from Fermina:

> At midnight he put on his Sunday suit and went to stand alone under Fermina Daza's balcony to play the love waltz he had composed for her, which was known only to the two of them and which for three years had been the emblem of their frustrated complicity. He played, murmuring the words, his violin bathed in tears, with an inspiration so intense that with the first measures the dogs on the street and then dogs all over the city began to howl, but then, little by little, they were quieted by the spell of the music, and the waltz ended in supernatural silence. (138)

Florentino reveals his eccentricity, by using all the resources of romantic tradition to court the woman who is the center of his interest. Serenade, poems, roses, love letters, perfume, all possible forms of compliment are transformed by a character who "could not avoid lyricism" (171), into an obsessive and singular form of communication.

Writing is one of his main strategies and it ranges from the telegraphic network he controls because of his work to the letters he writes, first as a personal expression and later, when he becomes the secretary of "unlettered lovers," as a clandestine profession allied to pretense and anonymity.

The world of Florentino is tinged by his exaltation of passion which parodies the self-centeredness of the romantic hero ("Florentino Ariza wrote everything with so much passion that even official documents seemed to be about love" [167]). He eventually becomes "involved in a feverish correspondence with himself" (172), sublimating his own sentimental energy by becoming an adviser to those in love: "he had so much love left over inside that he did not know what to do with it, and he offered it to unlettered lovers free of charge in the Arcade of Scribes" (171). But he is once again marginal and he practices a vicarious activity.

Along with commercial and amorous writing, he participates as a creative writer in the poetry competition and he also compiles a record in a coded book which is given the title "Women" and which recounts the story of his amorous adventures. There were "some twenty-five notebooks, with six hundred twenty-two entries of long-term liaisons, apart from the countless fleeting adventures that did not even deserve a charitable note" (152).

Florentino carries to the extreme attributes that are also present in other characters of the novel who are still marked by traces of romanticism. And it is he who actualizes the model that is developed in contrast to the dominant ideology of modernization. It is precisely this expansion of individualism and passion almost *ad infinitum*—the rebellion against social conventions and the impositions of age, the marginality assumed and transformed into a trump card by Florentino Ariza—that constitutes a counterpart to positivistic quantification and the exclusionary "progressiveness" of the elites.

In this disjunction, Fermina Daza represents a link that permits the confluence of those two visions of the world which, though in many ways incompatible, still never explode into open conflict. Daughter of a *nouveau riche* mule trader, a coarse man who is concerned with transforming her into a great lady, Fermina Daza consolidates her social situation by means of her marriage to Dr. Urbino. She thus enters a social circle that, however, never completely accepts her and that imposes its conventions on her. Because of her origin, her "untamed character," her tastes, her language, Fermina is always presented to the reader as a character who is identified with the popular sectors. Her social rank after her marriage with Urbino does not prevent her rejection by the upper-class families and her feeling of "always being in someone else's house" (207), nor her awareness of the fact that "[s]he had been caught up more quickly than she had believed in the tangle of conventions and prejudices of her new world" (208). The conflict with the manners and customs of the upper class is obvious:

> She was ashamed of their custom of setting the banquet table every day with embroidered table cloths, silver service, and funereal candelabra so that five phantoms could dine on *café con leche* and crullers. She detested the rosary at dusk, the affected table etiquette, the constant criticism of the way she held her silverware, the way she walked in mystical strides like a woman in the streets, the ways she dressed as if she were in the circus, and

even the rustic way she treated her husband and nursed her child without covering her breast with a mantilla. (207)

Although she shares her husband's way of life and throughout their marriage is a loyal companion, Fermina is "an irrational idolater of tropical flowers and domestic animals" (21), and up to the end rejects the oppressiveness of city life. Her ability to function—despite reservations—within the local elite and at the same time to understand the cede of anachronistic popular romanticism that is closely linked to national tradition makes her not only an intermediary between two social projects and two clearly differentiated lifestyles but also the privileged witness to the conflict between tradition and modernity that was part of that period of transition. Her upward social mobility also illustrates an inter-class dynamic that attenuates latent antagonisms, revealing the possibilities of order and coexistence that appeared at the beginning of the century as an indispensable requirement for the realization of the projects of the dominant class. Thus, the ritual manner in which she approaches Florentino during the commemorative mass for Juvenal Urbino in the cathedral signifies a transgression not only of convention but of the social boundaries:

> Throughout almost the whole ceremony, Fermina Daza stood in the family pew in front of the main altar, as elegant as when she attended the opera. But when it was over she broke with convention and did not stay in her seat, according to the custom of the day, to receive the spiritual award of condolences, but made her way instead through the crowd to thank each one of the guests: an innovative gesture that was very much in harmony with her style and character. Greeting one guest after another, she at last reached the pews of the poor relations, and then she looked around to make certain she had not missed anyone she knew. At that moment Florentino Ariza felt a supernatural wind lifting him out of himself: she had seen him. Fermina Daza moved away from her companions with the same assurance she brought to everything in society, held out her hand, and with a sweet smile, said to him:
> "Thank you for coming." (298)

TOWARDS A CRITIQUE OF MODERNITY

The final message of the novel is not however one of universal harmony. Rather it depicts "an unstable equilibrium" and a precarious correlation between the almost definitive breakdown of the romantic novel and its conjunction with modernity. Florentino is victorious in his quest as a survivor of a cultural system in open retreat, thanks to the fact that he had accepted his own marginality within a system that consistently relegated him to that position. Despite his outward appearance towards the end of the novel (bald, toothless, "a lame old man whose back burned with a burro's saddle sores" (327), he is nevertheless an example of defiant vitality and ready to affirm his rights to the end and even from the limits of the system and under the plague flag. He and Fermina are witnesses to the definitive collapse of the romantic framework on their final journey along a devastated river that was "only an illusion of memory":

> Captain Samaritano explained to them how fifty years of uncontrolled deforestation had destroyed the river: the boilers of the riverboats had consumed the thick forest of colossal trees that had oppressed Florentino Ariza on his first voyage. Fermina Daza would not see the animals of her dreams: the hunters for skins from the tanneries in New Orleans had exterminated the alligators that, with yawning mouths, had played dead for hours on end in the gullies along the shore as they lay in wait for butterflies, the parrots with their shrieking and the monkeys with their lunatic screams had died out as the foliage was destroyed, the manatees with their great breasts that had nursed their young and wept on the banks in a forlorn woman's voice were an extinct species, annihilated by the armored bullets of hunters for sport. (331)

The nostalgic and emotional tone of this evocative description reaffirms the value of a culture in which nature and the human are identified. The practical, the aesthetic and the moral appear increasingly as diverging paths determined by what—from a critical perspective on modernity—could be considered the supremacy of "instrumental reason." Everyday life is definitely colonized by new patterns of behaviour and values that mark a break with tradition. The practices of exploitation and economic penetration conveyed through images of violence are a sign of the new times: "In a few years, we'll ride the dry river bed in luxury automobiles" (337). The advent of modernity also includes political violence: "the larval wars that governments were bent on hiding with distracting decrees" (337) or the swollen bodies floating down the river that the captain is ordered to explain as victims of drowning accidents (336).

This progressive yet decadent vision of the end of the century is thus not homogeneous. Rather it is constituted thanks to the coexistence of social projects (one emergent and dominant, the other in retreat, linked to tradition and national values) which are intertwined like life and death at the beginning of the new century. The narrative achievement of *Love in the Time of Cholera* thus consists very largely in the representation of diverse forms of individual and collective consciousness articulated to the social imaginary by means of diverse cultural links and aesthetically dependent on the parody of the romantic code. Vitalism and rationalism, modernization and tradition, Europeanization and popular culture, integration and marginality thus constitute poles in an ideological complex basically composed of Utopian projects that raise the question of the imposition of or resistance to foreign models, a question that is still basic to contemporary nations.

With the affirmation, towards the end of the novel, that "it is life, more than death, than has no limits" (348), the novel seems also to raise the question of what life-forms Latin America has received from modernity. Clearly the text ultimately reveals cultural and ideological heterogeneity to be the characteristic of social development in the nations of Latin America, revealing the diversity of projects not only as ideological and political programs but also as differentiated forms of knowledge and deconstructions of reality. It is also evident that this heterogeneity does not imply pastiche (eclectic and uncritical coexistence), but rather the simultaneous existence of alternative projects, each one of which represents diverse sectorial interests and follows its own operative and representational logic.

In this sense the novel is, like other texts in the narrative saga of García Márquez, a reflection on power. Except that here, more than in his other works, underlying the pleasurable anecdotes that compose the novel, the ideological field is clearly marked. The dominant project alone enjoys the privilege of legality and it alone becomes institutionalized. Florentino achieves a late, private and clandestine happiness thanks to the persistence of an invincible subjectivity which achieves a relative victory on the margins of the system and at the very threshold of death. This treatment of a "limit situation" represented by the character who confronts change, the passage of time and conventions is significant. On the one hand, it is obvious that the work constitutes a reflection on the *social order* and, specifically, on the neopositivist and liberal rationalism that guided the organization of national states during the second half of the nineteenth and the beginning of the twentieth century. It is also evident that this reflection does not lead to a focalization of concrete and well-known aspects of the society represented, nor does it lead to an investigation of the basic causes that gave rise to the transition to modernity. Rather on various levels, it reveals the conflict between diverse articulations of the individual within the cultural horizon of the time. García Márquez projects this problem through the representation of a world fragmented not only by class stratification, but also by showing a process of cultural dismemberment that gradually transforms the social totality into a plurality of spheres (economic, political, moral, administrative, aesthetic, scientific, emotional [21]). The break that for García Márquez marks a new stage is not only between past and present but between the different areas that constitute social totality and which are in a process of disintegration. Each sphere functions according to its own logic in a world of increasing specialization and professionalization exemplified in the practices of both male characters. Through Urbino, medicine reveals its Messianic public task, its integration into the logical of modernization and progress; it is a universalizing practice that applies the formulae of a European model to a different reality, thus furthering to a great extent the breakup of national identity. In Florentino, "professionalism" takes the form of the extreme exploration and extension of his skills as an epistolary writer, lover and romantic hero who is integrated into the labor system under the principal rubric of the modernizing project—transport and communications. It is true that these sectors take on a parodic aspect that reinforces in him the idea of marginality and not of integration, and are more of a celebration of his eccentric and anachronic characteristics. The critique of modernity thus takes the form of loyalty to the past, to individualism, the questioning of the effects of modernizing praxis, and a defense of national identity.

By romanticizing the force of the tradition and the vitality of the popular sectors, by showing the delayed effect of an anachronistic individual heroism, by glorifying voluntarism and by relativizing the effects of marginalization, García Márquez depicts in a personal way the drama of modernity. The challenge of interpreting the real ideological implications of an America that has gradually taken shape in text after text of the continent's best known writer is left to the reader.

NOTES

1. On the theme of violence in the work of García Márquez, see, for example, Ernesto González Bermejo, "García Márquez: ahora doscientos años de soledad," in Peter Earle ed., *Gabriel García Márquez* (Madrid: Taurus, 1982); Angel Rama, "Un novelista de la Violencia latinoamericana," in Mario Benedetti et al., *Nueve asedios a García Márquez* (Santiago: Editorial Universitaria, 1972); Lucila Inés Mena, "*Cien años de soledad*: Novela de 'La Violencia'" *Hispamérica* 13 (April 1976): 3–23.

2. Page references are to Gabriel García Márquez, *Love in the Time of Cholera*, tr. Edith Grossman (New York: Alfred A. Knopf, 1989). Despite the vast bibliography on Gabriel García Márquez, there is as yet no global study of the Latin American question, that is, no exploration of what image of America is projected in his narratives, what are the ideological consequences of this "tropical" vision of history and the social reality of the

continent. However, new perspectives are opened by Victor Farias in *Los manuscritos de Melquíades. Cien años de soledad, burguesía latinoamericana y dialéctica de la reproducción ampliada de negación* (Frankfurt: Iberoamericana, 1981).

3. The phrase comes from Ricardo Gullón, "García Márquez o el olvidado arte de contar," in Peter Earle, *Gabriel García Márquez*.

4. Francisco Arroyo, "El amor, la vejez, la muerte" in *El País. Libros* 321 (Dec. 12, 1985): 2.

5. Arroyo, *El País*, mentions the links with Flaubert's *L'Education sentimentale*. The idea of the "mad hero" is developed by José Miguel Oviedo, who in several novels identifies as a prototype the individual who throws himself into a cause that enslaves and sometimes destroys him. See "*El amor en los tiempos de cólera* de Gabriel García Márquez", *Vuelta* 114 (Mayo, 1986): 33.

6. Oviedo, *Vuelta*, 37.

7. Arroyo, *El País*, 3.

8. In his *Teoritá de la novela* (Barcelona: Edhasa, 1971), 80, Georg Lukács privileges biography because of its organic structure. The relation between this organic and vital development of the "problematic hero" of the novel and the search for an ideal that exposes the system of concepts and values that motivates him may be applied to Florentino Ariza García Márquez, however, takes to the extreme of parody the possibilities of this genre.

9. Oviedo, *Vuelta*, 37.

10. Arroyo, *El País*, 2.

11. Arroyo, *El País*, 1.

12. Arroyo, *El País*, 2.

13. The association of love and plague is a tradition in literature, *Death in Venice* being one example. In Arroyo, *El País* (3), García Márquez also points out that plague was still common in the area described by the novel until the end of the last century.

14. René Girard's notion of triangulated desire is relevant here. See *Deceit, Desire and the Novel*, tr. Yvonne Freccero (Baltimore: The Johns Hopkins University Press, 1965), although it would have to be historicized in the case of the novel under discussion.

15. Bradford Burns, *The Poverty of Progress. Latin America in the Nineteenth Century* (Berkeley: University of California Press, 1980): 8–9.

16. Bradford Burns, *Poverty of Progress*, 17.

17. Bradford Burns, *Latin America. A Concise Interpretive History* (New York: Prentice Hall, 1982): 87.

JEAN FRANCO

Dr. Urbino's Parrot

W hen Gabriel García Márquez's *El amor en los tiempos del cólera* was first
published, several critics commented on its realism, as if the author had come
down to earth after a period of intoxication.[1] Indeed the novel with its class-
specific characters and attention to historical detail could pass for a
meticulous illustration of Lukács's theory of the historical novel (Moraña
1990, 27–43), although "the trade," writers of book jacket blurbs, critics and
the author himself, described it is a novel of love. ("There's so much to say
about the life of two people who love each other: It's infinite." [Interview
with Simons 1988, 48]). If this is the case, we might legitimately wonder
whether historical material serves any more purpose here than it does in *The
Name of the Rose* or *Shogun* where similar well-researched detail turned out to
be just the literary equivalent of a trompe l'oeil. Why would a Colombian
author in 1985 need to reconstruct in such detail the history of nineteenth-
century liberal reform in a Caribbean port city merely to provide a backdrop
to what *The Times* called the "unique Márquez magic of the sadness and
funniness of humanity"?[2] Is the novel realist or a pastiche of realism? Or is
it a Magritte-like text in which "copy" and "original" would be
indistinguishable were it not for a frame.

At first reading, *El amor* appears to be a far more transparent allegory

From *Indiana Journal of Hispanic Literatures* 1, no. 2 (Spring 1993) © 1993 by *Indiana Journal of
Hispanic Literatures*.

of the one hundred years of Colombian solitude than are García Márquez's previous novels, although his preferred historical period roughly speaking from the consolidation of the Colombian state to just before "la violencia"— seldom varies. The novel ends when the film version of *All Quiet on the Western Front* (released in 1930) is being shown, and it spans the hundred years of river boat and Atlantic steam navigation, in other words, a period in which the coastal regions of Colombia were more open to modernization and development than the interior. In this sense the novel provides an interesting comment on the incompatibility between the abstract post-Independence nation and the regional vernacular.

According to this realist reading, the two protagonists of the novel, the Paris-educated liberal reformer Dr. Urbino and the bastard son of a shipping company executive Florentino Ariza (who becomes the efficient manager of his uncle's river boat company), appear then as somewhat obvious and even mechanically symmetrical allegories, the one representing public spirited modernization, the other, native private enterprise. What undercuts such a reading is that two dystopian moments of stasis frame the optimistic rationalism of both Urbino and Florentino's public lives. The first occurs during Dr. Urbino's visit to the former slave quarters of the old colonial city, to see the mistress of a suicide. On this journey which he undertakes in an old-fashioned coach, he measures the distance between nostalgic memory and contemporary stagnation. The pestilence of the swamps "tantas veces idealizada por la nostalgia se convirtió en una realidad insoportable cuando el coche empezó a dar saltos por el lodazal de las calles donde los gallinazos se disputaban los desperdicios del matadero arrastrados por el mar de leva" (23). Although the mulattoes who "invade the beach" and the commercial area of the old viceregal quarter infuse "a la ciudad muerta un frenesí de feria humana olorosa a pescado frito: una vida nueva" (30), that new life is as much an index of decay as are flies on a corpse. The representation of nature as destructive of human endeavour is a common topos in modern Latin American literature. We recall the abandoned shipyard in Juan Carlos Onetti's novel of the same name (*El astillero*), the overgrown archaeological remains of Fushía's island in Mario Vargas Llosa's *La casa verde*, and the abandoned railway carriage in Augusto Roa Bastos's *El hijo del hombre*. In García Márquez's novel, it is the colonial city which seems to be caught in a time warp—"no le había ocurrido nada en cuatro siglos, salvo el envejecer despacio entre laureles marchitos y ciénagas podridas" (29)—which is in sharp contrast to the progress and modernity of the liberal city.

García Márquez's seamless prose weaves together Dr. Urbino's nostalgia for the old colonial city which he himself had helped to destroy and which now persists as "an illusion of memory." Indeed, it is not easy to distinguish between the author's and Dr. Urbino's nostalgia, especially as the colonial city has all the usual García Márquez indexes of class stratification—the drunken frenzied carnaval of the poor and the enclosed puritanical lives of the impoverished upper classes.

> Sus amores eran lentos y difíciles, perturbados a menudo por presagios siniestros, y la vida les parecía interminable. Al anochecer, en el instante opresivo del tránsito, se alzaba de las ciénagas una tormenta de zancudos carniceros, y una tierna vaharada de mierda humana, cálida y triste, revolvía en el fondo del alma la certidumbre de la muerte. (30)

Nostalgia emanates from the residue not only of the past but of the past-within-the-present, a past that the liberal city has excreted.

The author provides the reader with a brief historical synthesis of the history of the port. It was here that the treasure fleets had gathered before setting sail for Spain and here that the slave markets flourished. Independence and liberal reform brought not so much a transformation as a displacement. The old unreformed colonial city has been left to the marginalized. It has become a "death trap of the poor," no more than an "illusion of memory" to those who like Dr. Urbino have moved to more hygienic quarters. The novel thus envisions modernization as a spatial rearrangement rather than an evolution: the old city shelters the excreted residue that is not needed for the progress of the elite who are, by the very fact of spatial distance, able to "inhabit another time." García Márquez's novel thus seems to be structured around a now familiar juxtaposition of tradition and modernity, popular excess and bourgeois temperance.

Dr. Urbino himself is the agent of modernization, having successfully eradicated cholera on his return from his medical studies in Europe. The cleansing and reform of the modern city made it possible for the elite to live as if they were coeval with Europe. The ghettoization of the poor removed them physically from the "gente decente," and their carefully controlled cultural world of chamber concerts, poetry festivals, and modernist design. Fin de siècle high culture and rationalism expelled popular culture and religion (superstition) from the polis—which allowed the lettered city to exist as if disembodied while the poor, to use Foucault's term, enjoyed their heterotopia of compensation (1984).

Although the Caribbean port city had been linked to Europe since the colonial period, its connection with the interior is far more precarious. The hinterland is wild and untamed, except for the banana plantations which form a separate enclave. It is only when Dr. Urbino and his wife take a balloon flight to celebrate the beginning of the new century that they have a panoramic view, of territories that are adjacent to their own.

> Volaron sobre los palafitos de las Trojas de Cataca, pintados de colores de locos, con tambos para criar iguanas de comer, y colgajos de balsaminas y astromelias en los jardines lacustres.... Volaron sobre el océano de sombras de los plantíos de banano, cuyo silencio se elevaba hasta ellos como un vapor letal. (296)

From the vantagepoint of the balloon, and with the aid of a spyglass, Urbino sees the corpses of plantation workers shot through the back of the head. This panoptic vision made possible by modern technology clearly shows the way that national space is distributed—"differentiated"—in Neil Smith's words, "according to the territorial division of labor" (105–113).

This careful mapping of spatial and social differentiation is a commonplace of García Márquez's novels in which the heterotopia of compensation is juxtaposed with exploited enclaves such as the banana plantations which, in turn, are carefully insulated from the administrative and cultural reach of the city. It is only when the boundaries are crossed that the illusion of memory is exposed.

This vision/memory of decay is mirrored in an episode towards the end of the novel when the once fertile river along which Florentino Ariza travels is also described as "an illusion of memory." The echoing of this phrase pairs the protagonists who are perhaps not so much opponents as different aspects of the same process. The second vision of ruin is, however, even more devastating than the first. The river boat on which Ariza and Fermina Daza consummate their long postponed love affair passes along the now desolate shores of the River Magdalena. Although the boat is a private space protected from the intrusion of the outside world by the cholera flag (thus creating a miniature heterotopia), devastation surrounds it. In collusion with the captain, the couple plan to go on sailing up and down the river till the end of their lives, between the ocean and a place that is called, not El Dorado (the Golden Man) but La Dorada (the Gilded Woman) and which is now the railway terminus that connects the river to the capital city, Bogotá.

It is easy to read some romantic triumph of love into this ending but there are deeper ironies in the situation. After writing his novel *El general en su laberinto*, García Márquez confessed that he had been attracted at first more by the river Magdalena than by the figure of Bolívar because having been born on the Caribbean coast he had travelled the route since childhood. "En mis años de estudiante lo recorrí once veces en sus dos sentidos, en aquellos buques de vapor que salían de los astilleros de Misisipi condenados a la nostalgia, y con una vocación mítica que ningún escritor podría resistir" (Simons 48).

"Nostalgia," a familiar word in García Márquez's vocabulary, marks a history that is distorted in memory, is unrepeatable and therefore associated with mourning for something that is forever lost.[3] Yet this very nostalgia stirs those who are agents of the destruction of nature. In *El general en su laberinto*, Bolívar already forecasts the river's fate: "se notaban ya los primeros destrozos hechos por la tripulaciones de los buques de vapor para alimentar las calderas" and he utters the prophetic words, "los peces tendrán que aprender a caminar sobre la tierra porque las aguas se acabarán" (1989, 99–100). But in the course of Florentino's lifetime, the boat's passengers have killed off the wild life and the boat engines have consumed the forest; the once fertile river banks are no more than an "illusion of memory." Whereas the dissolution of the colonial city had been slow and entropic, the death of the river is swift and irreparable. It is in this terminal scenery that love triumphs. Nevertheless, as in his other novels, García Márquez's deeply pessimistic outlook has been cleverly camouflaged by the rapid surface motion of the narrative which forestalls but cannot overcome death.

Given this vision, it is not surprising that this apparently jovial novel begins with suicide and closes with the death of nature:

> [L]os cazadores de pieles de las tenerías de Nueva Orleans habían exterminado los caimanes que se hacían los muertos con las fauces abiertas durante horas y horas en los barrancos de la orilla para sorprender a las mariposas, los loros con sus algarabías y los micos con sus gritos de locos se habían ido muriendo a medida que se les acababan las frondas, los manatíes de grandes tetas de madres que amamantaban a sus crías y lloraban con voces de mujer desolada en los playones eran una especie extinguida por las balas blindadas de los cazadores de placer. (479)

Yet what is most interesting about the novel is the way that the good-hearted protagonists contribute unwittingly to destruction. Urbino's sanitary reforms enable modernization in the form of consumer culture; Florentino efficiently runs the riverboat company which destroys the river. The relationship between modernization and transport and communication is explained in a blatantly authorial paragraph:

> Un viajero inglés de principios de siglo xix, refiriéndose al viaje combinado en canoa y en mula, que podía durar hasta cincuenta jornadas, había escrito: "Este es uno de los peregrinajes más

> malos e incómodos que un ser humano pueda realizar." Esto
> había dejado de ser cierto los primeros ochenta años de la
> navegación a vapor, y luego había vuelto a serlo para siempre,
> cuando los caimanes se comieron la última mariposa, y se
> acabaron los manatíes maternales, se acabaron los loros, los
> micos, los pueblos: se acabó todo. (437)

The irony here is, of course, that the very effort which made modernization
possible destroys natural wealth. The aporia around which this and other
novels of García Márquez are constructed is the impossibility in a class-and-
race stratified society of combining modernization with some form of
organic development. Not surprisingly literature then becomes a register of
loss, and nostalgia. But by the end of the novel even this tenuous nostalgia
seems to be vanquished by the death of nature which, of course, also involves
the death of romantic and positivistic visions that are as closely linked as the
two protagonists by having nature (woman) as their object. García Márquez's
own comments on the novel do not support this reading. Although he
confesses his fascination with the river, he also insists that he did not want
the description of its destruction to overshadow the relationship between the
lovers; he explains away Florentino's lifelong indifference to the fate of the
river whose ruin he only consciously registers when it is too late, by the fact
that he was blinded by passion, saying that Florentino "is very selfish as all
men are" (Simons 48). What remains unsaid, however, is that this
"selfishness" cannot be disassociated from the ethical problem of capitalism
in dependent societies in which there are often no political constraints on
irresponsible power.

The novel is, however, more than an appeal on behalf of endangered
species. The consummated love affair between the aged Florentino and
Fermina draws attention to the novel's coupling of romanticism and the
practical, of private life and private enterprise. Romance is not incompatible
with instrumental reason but locked in its deadly embrace. Florentino Ariza's
inventive eroticism does not prevent him from being a competent manager
of the riverboat company. Urbino's provincial modernity does not conflict
with his Catholic domestic code. The two men whose temperaments are
apparently so diverse, function within the same system of values, a system
which separates work from personal life and allows personal satisfaction and
desire to be considered an unalloyed good. This is, of course, applicable to
our own time and underlies the whole valorization of private life and
personal satisfaction. Urbino and Florentino are blind and unwitting agents
in a destruction that occurs despite the best of intentions and even because
of the drive for personal happiness.

García Márquez's meticulous reconstruction of a system that twins romanticism with positivism is thus functional to a plot that carries to the extreme the idea of postponed gratification. The pleasure of reading *El amor*, is inseparably linked to this desire for and postponement of consummation. ("The most wonderful thing would be if they could go on loving forever" [Simons 48].) And, as is generally the case, romance tends to control and subordinate those bleaker elements which might make us reflect a little more carefully on contemporary ascesis.

This brings me back to my original question of what it means to rewrite the "realist" narrative of history at a time when "master narratives" no longer seem to work, neither the narrative of the nation's cultural autonomy based on its pristine nature nor the narrative of the supersession of individualism that nineteenth-century realism often deployed. At the same time, the novel clearly does not parody realism, although it can be described as non-antagonistic imitation or pastiche, a pastiche moreover, that lacks any framing or distancing device of the order of "this is not a pipe," or, more appropriately, "this is not *Nostromo*." What makes it "not *Nostromo*" is our temporal distance from the events, from the naive nineteenth-century liberalism which in the time of cynical reason we are being asked to relive as if it had never happened or as if we are ignorant of its outcome. It seems at best disingenuous of García Márquez to feed the consumer demand for happy endings while showing that he is perfectly aware that the unhappy ending has already occurred. In this sense the novel recalls some of the neofigurist paintings (which refer to realism) described by Fredric Jameson (170–180). The novel's insistence on repetition, copying and imitation can indeed be read as the corollary of and commentary on the present recycling of neoliberalism.

That is why the parrot is a significant character in the novel and it is not incidental that it is introduced into Urbino's household by his wife and that it causes his death. García Márquez always distributes gender attributes along conventional lines so it is not surprising that women should be associated with nature. Fermina likes to collect exotic species. Collecting is, of course, already an indication of the end of nature (or at least of the idea of nature as unproduced and unrelated to human activity) since collections juxtapose creatures or objects which would not normally co-exist in the same habitat. In Fermina's case this cohabitation leads to disaster for her rabid German mastiff (obviously a foreigner to the country) attacks the menagerie, leaving "a marsh of blood." Urbino has the surviving exotica killed and their bodies burned in an isolated field. He then lays down the law, "nothing that does not speak will come into this house," thus drawing an ideological boundary between the human world which possesses language and the animal, in other words creating the Other as those who do not speak. Fermina finds an unsatisfactory substitute for her love of nature in the form of illustrations from Linnaeus's Natural History which she frames and hangs on the drawing room walls. As Mary Louise Pratt points out, Linnaeus founded a planetary system by means of which hitherto unknown or uncatalogued species could be classified in whatever part of the world they were found (24–37). In García Márquez's novel, however, the Linnaeus illustrations are substitutes for an absent referent—the natural life which is already on the verge of extinction. This extinction, however, does nothing to invalidate the cataloguing system itself which has nothing to say about the survival of species.

But the Linnaeus illustrations cannot altogether satisfy Fermina who finds a way of transgressing Urbino's rule by buying the parrot, a creature that possesses speech or, at least, the simulacrum of speech. The parrot, deplumed to stop it from flying away, is also nothing if not perverse; it is "maniacal" for it speaks not on request but only "en las ocasiones menos pensadas, pero entonces lo hacía con una claridad y un use de razón que no eran muy comunes en los seres humanos" (34). He had been tutored by Dr. Urbino himself ("y eso le había valido privilegios que nadie tuvo nunca en la familia, ni siquiera los hijos cuando eran niños" [34]). It is *as if* the parrot were human and it is this mistake which leads to Dr. Urbino's death.

Although never made explicit in the novel, the parrot has a history. When Columbus reached the Antilles on his first voyage, he accepted gifts of parrots to take back to Spain. It was a sign that he had touched the non-Western world. In his novel, *El otoño del patriarca*, García Márquez included a comic parody in which the dictator looks out of his window, anachronically sees the fifteenth-century Spanish caravelles and notices that his subjects are all wearing red bonnets, and carrying the beads and the bells that Columbus had brought as gifts. There follows a comic account from the native's point of view, of the arrival of the Spaniards, mocking their surprise at sight of naked bodies and their "cambalache de puta madre"; in no time at all,

> todo el mundo estaba cambalachando sus loros, su tabaco, sus bolas de chocolate, sus huevos de iguana, cuanto Dios crió, pues de todo tomaban y daban de aquello que tenían de buena voluntad, y hasta querían cambiar a uno de nosotros por un jubón de terciopelo para mostrarnos en las Europas. (45)

The direct citation from Columbus's letters ("tomaban y daban de aquello que tenían de buena voluntad") is resemanticized when parroted by the supposedly uncomprehending natives; it is also significant that parrots which are exotic to the Europeans but commonplace to the natives are among the articles exchanged in this first encounter. Urbino's parrot thus carries a freight of messages from this remote past, innocently introducing into the lives of "gente decente" the epistemic violence of conquest. Thus, "en las tardes de lluvia, cuando se le desataba la lengua por la alegría de las plumas ensopadas, decía frases de otros tiempos que no había podido aprender en la casa, y que permitía pensar que era también mas viejo de lo que parecía" (38–39). It was a parrot of Paramaribo "que sólo sabía decir blasfemias de marineros, pero que las decía con una voz tan humana que bien valía su precio excesivo de doce centavos" (38). It is this ability to simulate the human that distracts attention from the violence of the encounter which might otherwise have disturbed Urbino's domestic peace.

In Julian Barnes's *Flaubert's Parrot*, Flaubert's stuffed bird allows the narrator to speak of what might otherwise be unspeakable. In Vargas Llosa's *El hablador*, the wounded "storyteller" is friended by parrots in the jungle, so discovering that his animal spirit is a parrot (which is perhaps rather too obvious a parallel).[4] In these novels the parrots are stage props. In García Márquez's novel, the parrot is a living embodiment of the power of "colonial" mimicry to ridicule hegemonic discourse although this mimicry often seems more like the last squawk of spontaneous freedom than the triumphant signifying of an emergent culture.

The doctor is a strong believer in the reforming powers of pedagogy and teaches the parrot Latin and correct French. From somewhere it has also acquired political slogans such as "Long Live the Liberal Party, dammit" "un grito temerario que les había costado la vida a más de cuatro borrachitos felices" (40). It imitates the fashionable French music hall songs that are played on the phonograph and when thieves break into the house, it mimics the mastiff's barks "que no habrían sido tan verosímiles si hubieran sido reales, y gritando rateros, rateros, rateros dos gracias salvadoras que no había aprendido en la casa" (39). The parrot, indeed, knows a lot of things that could not have been learned in the bourgeois household. In its travels it has acquired different speech genres, high and low culture, upper-class and lower class language. In what hierarchy of value or what single enunciation can one place Latin, correct French, sentimental songs, the barking of a dog, the cries of an outraged victim, and dockland language? Not only this but the bird is able to reproduce both performance (of music hall songs) and reception (the laughter of servant girls). The parrot registers speech genres and vocabulary which are transformed in their travels from one continent to another and from one region to another, from tragic to comic, from sentiment to mockery. It is precisely the social and cultural boundaries that separate the Paris music hall and classroom pedagogy, correct French and the laughter of servants, that the parrot transgresses.

When, after mimicking the French music hall tenors and sopranos, the parrot also imitates the servant girls' pleasure in the performance, it not only registers the presence of the subaltern and the gulf between copy and original but also exposes elite pretensions. The sentimental associations that bind the elite to Europe are exposed to parody and the border patrol of class stratification disregarded. The parrot scrambles communication and education (the twin liberal shibboleths) because it has the freedom of the asocial.

This is the difference between the parrot and the institutional forms of mimesis and copying which inform the culture of the two protagonists. Urbino's death as he tries to capture the escaped parrot is duly recorded by a European painter who paints

> un lienzo gigantesco de un realismo patético, en el que se veía al doctor Urbino subido en la escalera y en el instante mortal en que extendió la mano para atrapar al loro. Lo único que contrariaba la cruda verdad de su historia era que no llevaba en el cuadro la camisa sin cuello y los tirantes de rayas verdes, sino el sombrero hongo y la levita de paño negro de un grabado de prensa de los años del cólera. (76)

Unconsciously the painter anticipates Magritte in placing the bowler hatted gentleman in this absurd situation. Realism is revealed to be a copy of a copy but one that never quite reproduces the original. The painting is later burned by art students "as a symbol of an aesthetic and a time they despised."

In art and literature, there is only a slender line between imitation, ridicule and the ridiculous. At the Golden Orchid Poetry festival which Florentino enters anonymously because Fermina officiates, the prize goes to a Chinese immigrant. He had written

> un soneto de la más pura estirpe parnasiana, perfecto, atravesado por una brisa de inspiración. La única explicación posible era que algún poeta de los grandes hubiera concebido aquella broma para burlarse de los Juegos Florales, y que el chino se había prestado a ella con la determinación de guardar el secreto hasta la muerte. (254–55)

The enigma is never resolved. The Chinese is buried with the Golden Orchid in his coffin.

> Con motivo de la muerte se evocó en la prensa el incidente olvidado de los Juegos Florales, se reprodujo el soneto con una

viñeta modernista de doncellas turgentes con cornucopias de oro,
y los dioses custodios de la poesía se valieron de la ocasión para
poner las cosas en su puesto: el soneto le pareció tan malo a la
nueva generación, que ya nadie puso en duda que en realidad
fuera escrito por el chino muerto. (255)

Whereas the parrot's mimicry comes from oral tradition, literary and artistic imitation cannot overcome the dynamics of artistic production which since Romanticism has been powered by change and renewal. Urbino's portrait suffers the same fate as the Chinese poet for the "faithful" homage of one generation is mocked by the next. Art and literature share the fate of the commodity. And Florentino is just as much a copier as the more conventional Urbino—literally so since he writes love letters for the illiterate. Even his poetry is not original. One day he finds in his father's notebooks a line that had been written many years before he was born and which he thought he himself had composed "Lo único que me duele de morir es que no sea de amor" (223).

The novel continually draws attention to an area of slippage, the impossibility of either originality or of faithful copying because the metropolitan text can never be properly reproduced in a dependent context. This is, of course, scarcely a new idea. Martí, a century ago, was critical of the "imported book" and Machado de Assis parodied "travelling theories" brilliantly, in *Epitaph for a Small Winner*. García Márquez, on the other hand is writing with the benefit of hindsight and in the wake of modernism and the avant garde's obsession with the new and when the pastiche of historical texts in fictional form has become commonplace.[5] Indeed, the Brazilian writer and critic, Silviano Santiago has described Latin American literature as always being a deliberate rewriting of other texts and thus as essentially pastiche, parody and translation (1976). *El amor en los tiempos del cólera* would seem to confirm this insight. But the pastiche of realism can also be read as an index of the end of the 'high' narrative of the continent's cultural originality of which *Cien años de soledad* seemed to be the culmination. The rewriting of the metropolitan realist text is double edged, foregrounding on the one hand cultural lag (despite his aspirations, Urbino is never entirely coeval with the metropolis) and the elite's exclusion of subaltern cultures which clearly do not imitate the metropolis. Also, unlike the Indian imperial subject described by Homi Bhabha on whom hybridisation is imposed by an occupying power, the Latin American elites were willing agents of metropolitan authority, carrying out a process of secularization that deprived popular religion, language and memory of any place in the public sphere (93–122).

In an article on García Márquez, Kumkum Sangari makes a case for not reading fatalism into García Márquez use of repetition and circularity. Arguing that, unlike Western modernism, García Márquez's marvellous is the product of a historical situation, she claims that "the power of Márquez's narratives lies in the insistent pressure of *freedom* as the *absent* horizon—which is neither predictable nor inevitable" (1987). To be sure her essay is based on García Márquez's two major novels, *Cien años de soledad* and *El otoño del patriarca* and not on the more pedestrian *El amor en los tiempos del cólera* and *El general en su laberinto*. But it is interesting to examine the "politics of the possible" in the light of two novels in which the horizon is not so much absent as a simulacrum. After all, we know that the pristine Magdalena river is non-reproducible, that Fermina and Florentino's journey is not interminable and that Bolivar will not have a second chance. In these novels, the stripping away of marvellous realism forces the stark recognition not of the politics of the possible but of the anti-ethics of individualism. Florentino's selfishness and (in Thomas Pynchon's words [1988]) his amorality, and Urbino's bourgeois civility are both an anti-ethics because they are based on privilege.

Commenting on the development of individualism in the seventeenth century, C.B. Macpherson remarks that "the individual was seen neither as a moral whole, nor as a part of a larger social whole, but as owner of himself. The relation of ownership, having become for more and more men the critically important relation determining their actual freedom and actual prospect of realizing their full potentialities, was read back into the nature of the individual" (3). This could very well stand for a description of "character" in García Márquez's novels with one proviso. As I pointed out in a previous essay, the idea of realizing one's full potentialities becomes mere idiosyncracy in societies in which social projects rarely outlast the span of human life (1976, 4–16).

But this is an old topic in Latin American literature (*La muerte de Artemio Cruz* was published in 1962); what seems different about *El amor en los tiempos del cólera* is that nature except in its parasitic aspects can no longer regenerate for, to quote Fredric Jameson, "the *other* of our societies is no longer Nature at all" (35). The extraordinary vision of, for example, Caribbean sea-life in Alejo Carpentier's *El siglo de las luces* or García Márquez's selva in *Cien años de soledad* no longer has any ground except in fantasy. The whole basis on which marvellous realism was posited—that the marvellous is the real in Latin America—has become a simulacrum. A poetics of the new cedes, to the bleaker realities of reiterating the past in order to demonstrate the sterility of the enterprise. Like a hall of mirrors, *El amor en los tiempos del cólera* reflects only a reflection. Only now there seems to be nothing outside the hall.

Perhaps because of its transparency, the novel illuminates an often-ignored aspect of García Márquez's writing. Ebullience and hedonism mask the ascesis—the withdrawal into the private world. In earlier novels this often signalled the fact that there was no viable public sphere so that the individual became an eccentric and an exotic within his own society. In *El amor en los tiempos del cólera*, however, the ethical problem surfaces with a vengeance. Whereas in nineteenth-century realism, private and public good were closely associated so that individual blemishes were registered on the social body, García Márquez's novel deploys realist allegory to quite different ends, showing the incompatibility between private and public good. The fact that this sounds like a mere piety says something about our global culture in which literature has been cut loose from the responsibility that figured so prominently in the cultural discourse of the sixties, leaving only sedentary nostalgia.

NOTES

1. For instance, Thomas Pynchon "The Heart's Eternal Vow."
2. Quoted on the back of the English translation, *Love in the Time of Cholera*, tr. Edith Grossman (London: Penguin Books, 1989).
3. On postmodern nostalgia see Jameson, especially page 170.
4. [In Macunaíma, a parrot ends up as the only one who still speaks the hero's language and actually preserves his story for the author-editor Mario de Andrade to pass on to us readers. In native terms, the creature is credited with notable powers: cf. Fig. 4. Ed. Note]
5. See Franco, 1990, 95–107.

WORKS CITED

Bhabha, Homi. "Representation and the Colonial Text: A Critical Exploration of Some Forms of Mimeticism." In *The Theory of Reading*. Ed. Frank Gloversmith. Sussex: Harvester Press, New Jersey: Barnes & Noble Books, 1984.

Foucault, Michel. "Des espaces autres." *Architecture Mouvement-Continuité*. Paris: October, 1984.

Franco, Jean. "Pastiche in Contemporary Latin American Literature." *Studies in 20th Century Literature* 14.1 (1990): 95–107.

———. "The Limits of the Liberal Imagination: *Nostromo* and *One Hundred Years of Solitude*." *Punto de Contacto* (1976): 4–16.

García Márquez, Gabriel. *Amor en tiempos de cólera*. Buenos Aires: Sudamericana, 2 ed. 1985.

———. *El general en su laberinto*. Madrid: Mondadori, 1989.

———. *El otoño del patriarca*. Barcelona: Plaza y Janés, 1975.

Jameson, Fredric. *Postmodernism or, The Cultural Logic of Late Capitalism*. Durham, NC: Duke UP, 1991.

Lukács, Georg. *The Theory of the Novel*. Trans. Anna Bostock. Cambridge, Mass.: M.I.T. Press, 1971.

Macpherson, C.B. *The Political Theory of Possessive Individualism.* Oxford: Oxford UP, 1962.

Moraña, Mabel. "Modernity and Marginality in *Love in the Time of Cholera.*" *Studies in 20th Century Literature* 14.1 (1990): 27–43.

Pratt, Mary Louise. *Imperial Eyes: Travel Writing and Transculturation.* London and New York: Routledge, 1992.

Pynchon, Thomas. "The Heart's Eternal Vow," *The New York Times Book Review* (April 10, 1988).

Sangari, Kum Kum. "The Politics of the Possible." *Cultural Critique* 7 (Fall 1987).

Santiago, Silviano. "O Entre-lugar do discurso latino-americano." *Uma literatura nos tropicos. Ensaios sobre dependencia cultural.* São Paulo: Editora perspectiva, 1976.

Simons, Marlise. "The Best Years of his Life: An Interview with Gabriel García Márquez," *The New York Times Book Review* (April 10,1988): 48.

Smith, Neil. *Uneven Development: Nature, Capital and the Production of Space.* Oxford: Basil Blackwood, 1984.

Vargas Llosa, Mario. *El hablador.* Barcelona: Plaza y Janés, 1975.

M. KEITH BOOKER

The Dangers of Gullible Reading:
Narrative as Seduction in García Márquez'
Love in the Time of Cholera

Initial critical reaction to Gabriel García Márquez' *Love in the Time of Cholera* has been positive, even rhapsodic, and most readers have found the book to be an uplifting affirmation of the human spirit, the author's kindest and gentlest work. Gene Bell-Villada is typical: even while recognizing that overly romantic attitudes are sometimes the subject of satire in the book, he still concludes that *Love* is basically "a good old-fashioned love story" (191). Indeed, Bell-Villada goes on to applaud García Márquez for his "courage and originality in writing a novel of love (a subject traditionally thought of as the preserve of younger authors) when on the verge of old age" (202). But *Love* is a complex work, and as García Márquez himself has said of it in an interview, "you have to be careful not to fall into my trap" (Williams 136). *Love in the Time of Cholera* is indeed a novel of love, but it is also much more, and Mabel Moraña probably gets closer to the heart of the matter when she suggests that it is "like other texts in the narrative saga of García Márquez, a reflection on power" (40).

The theme of love in the novel focuses on the lifelong fascination of Florentino Ariza with Fermina Daza, a fascination that is strongly informed by Ariza's own excessively romantic attitude toward life. This attitude derives largely from Ariza's gullible reading of bad literature, and the echo here of Flaubert's *Madame Bovary* is surely more than accidental. But there are more

From *Studies in Twentieth-Century Literature* 17, no. 2 (Summer 1993). © 1993 *Studies in Twentieth Century Literature*.

links between the texts of Flaubert and of García Márquez than this obvious one. In particular, the association with Flaubert provides a useful entry point into *Love* as a meditation on power as well as an exploration of romanticism. Near the end of *Madame Bovary* the sinister and self-promoting pharmacist Homais compiles a list of the credentials that he believes qualify him for the cross of the Legion of Honor, which he will in fact eventually win. Among these accomplishments, he congratulates himself for the "devotion" he showed doing his professional duty "in the time of the cholera" (253).[1] Perhaps one should not make too much of the fact that García Márquez verbally echoes this passage from Flaubert in the title of his novel, especially as the title functions on a number of levels within García Márquez' own text.[2] The echo may even be coincidental. But in the richly intertextual work of García Márquez such correspondences often bear surprising fruit when harvested carefully, even when the seeds have not originally been planted by the author. For example, García Márquez himself has identified "allusions" in *One Hundred Years of Solitude* to works he had not even read at the time he wrote his book (Janes 7). In any case, it is clear that *Madame Bovary* is of major importance as a source for *Love*, and the illumination provided by reading García Márquez through Flaubert is considerably enriched by bringing Homais into the picture, since Flaubert's manipulative pharmacist-vulgarian calls attention to the quests for power and domination that constitute a central theme of García Márquez' novel as well.

Most obviously, Homais is a representative of the philistine impulses that Flaubert so abhorred in the society of his contemporary France. But more than that, he is a generalized figure of the bad aspects of Enlightenment thinking. He prides himself on his education, his knowledge, and his scientific approach to things, and—following the Baconian dictum that "knowledge is power"—he puts his talents to use in furthering his own ambitions and in manipulating those around him for his own ends. As such he recalls the critique of Enlightenment thinking put forth by Max Horkheimer and Theodor Adorno in *The Dialectic of Enlightenment*. Horkheimer and Adorno suggest that the scientific impetus of the Enlightenment is informed by a quest not for a liberating truth, but for a power that ultimately enslaves: "What men want to learn from nature is how to use it in order to wholly dominate it and other men" (*Dialectic* 4). In particular, they suggest that the emphasis on the power of the individual in Enlightenment thought is related to a drive to dominate nature, a drive that inevitably turns back upon itself and leads to the formation of individuals who are internally repressed and of societies consisting of individual subjects who strive for domination of each other.

The Horkheimer/Adorno critique of the Enlightenment is also clearly relevant to the concerns of García Márquez' fiction. In *One Hundred Years of Solitude* José Arcadio Buendía insists on putting the scientific knowledge of the gypsy Melquíades to work for practical technological use, but his attempts to dominate nature through science invariably fail—and often in ways that recall Horkheimer and Adorno quite directly. For example, when José Arcadio attempts to use the gypsy's magnets to locate gold he finds instead an ancient suit of Spanish armor, with its associated echoes of imperial domination. In general, the citizens of Macondo find technological progress to be not liberating, but enslaving.[3] Science and technology also figure as negative forces in *Love*, particularly in the way that technological "progress" has led to the degradation of Colombia's natural environment and to the destruction of the Great Magdalena River that figures so centrally in the book. But García Márquez is no Luddite, and his argument is not with technological progress per se.[4] Instead, the link to Horkheimer and Adorno (courtesy of Flaubert's Homais) indicates that the real target of García Márquez' criticisms of the negative side of progress is the kind of ideology of domination that informs not only Enlightenment science, but a whole variety of other mechanisms of power as well, including imperialism, totalitarianism, and the Latin American tradition of *machismo*. A look at *Love* through the optic of these issues shows a book far more complex than the sweetly sentimental love story it is often perceived to be.

The character in *Love* whom Homais resembles most is Dr. Juvenal Urbino. Urbino is, on the surface at least, a rather admirable figure, if a little stiff and conventional. He is intelligent, educated, successful, an image of the kind of enlightened man who might bring hope of a better life to the benighted inhabitants of García Márquez' fictionalized Colombia. But a comparison with Homais helps to reveal certain ominous cracks and fissures in the surface of this depiction of Urbino. For example, one begins to wonder whether Urbino's rise to social and professional prominence might partake of some of the ruthlessly self-serving ambition that drives Homais onward toward the cross of the Legion of Honor. Indeed, Urbino himself is not above accepting honors, including being granted the rank of Commander in that same Legion (43). Finally, especially if Homais is read through Horkheimer and Adorno, aspects of Urbino's character such as the fact that he is so thoroughly "in control of his nature" begin to take on undertones of a drive for domination that may inform all of the good doctor's activities (105).

When we first meet Urbino at the beginning of the book we learn that he is a man very much accustomed to being in charge of whatever situation he may encounter. He arrives on the scene of the suicide of his friend Jeremiah de Saint-Amour, bullies the police inspector, and orders that the press be told that the death occurred due to natural causes (5–6). These actions, of course, can be interpreted as a perfectly understandable attempt to protect the memory of his friend, though it is telling that Urbino refuses to intercede with the Archbishop so that Saint-Amour can be buried on holy ground. And Urbino shows another negative side to his character when he reads Saint-Amour's suicide note and learns that his friend had been not a political exile as he had thought, but an escaped convict. Further, he discovers that Saint-Amour had been carrying on a clandestine sexual relationship for years. These revelations offend Urbino's self-righteous sense of propriety, and he shows not understanding, but disgust, rejecting his friend's memory. And when Urbino's wife Fermina Daza expresses sympathy for the dead Saint-Amour, Urbino violently explains to her the reason for his revulsion: "What infuriates me is not what he was or what he did, but the deception he practiced on all of us for so many years" (32). In short, what angers Urbino is the knowledge that he has been duped, that he has not been so thoroughly in charge of matters as he has believed—and of course there is the irony of the fact that Urbino himself has a past clandestine sexual history of which he may not want to be reminded.

Being in charge is clearly important to Urbino. Though he conducts numerous civic projects that are to the benefit of the local community it is not at all clear that he does so out of purely selfless motives. He does not hesitate, for example, to utilize the fire department that he has organized on European models for personal needs such as catching his escaped parrot. Urbino shows his typical imperious style when he sends for the firemen: "Tell them it's for me," he says (25). Indeed, in looking at Urbino's organization of the fire department one might keep in mind that Flaubert's Homais tops off the list of his own projects with which he lays claim to the cross of the Legion of Honor by noting that "there is always the assistance I give at fires!" (253).

It is also worth noting that not just the fire department, but all of Urbino's innovations tend to be based on European models. In *Love*, as in *One Hundred Years of Solitude*, scientific knowledge is something that comes to Colombia from tho outside, as a sign of European technical and cultural superiority. But García Márquez consistently suggests in his work that such European imports often result not in improvement, but in degradation of living conditions in Colombia. The local aristocracy in *Love* are mocked for their fascination with European consumer goods (an image of foreign economic domination), even though those goods may be useless and out of place in Latin America. On her various trips to Europe even the practical Fermina Daza buys massive amounts of commodities in an attempt (again echoing Emma Bovary) to fill the emptiness in her life. Most of these goods (like heavy European coats) simply get stored in trunks and closets when she returns to Colombia. And García Márquez indicates the dehumanizing impact of this invasion of commodities in Fermina's own attitude: "she was dismayed by the voracity with which objects kept invading living spaces, displacing the humans, forcing them back into corners" (301).

In this vein it is important to note that, though Urbino reads extensively, he has no interest in the literature of his native Latin America. Instead, he read the latest books ordered from Paris and Madrid, "although he did not follow Spanish literature as closely as French" (8). This sense of disengagement from his local context perhaps shows up most clearly in Urbino's style of dealing with the local cholera epidemics that he must combat in the course of his professional duties. Urbino's father Dr. Marco Aurelio Urbino had become so passionately and personally involved in the treatment of cholera victims that he himself contracted the disease and died from it (112–13). After this death, Juvenal Urbino becomes obsessed with battling against cholera, the very existence of which seems to stand as an affront to his personal mastery and as a challenge to his ability to dominate nature through science. Urbino shows a strong disdain for his father's methods, "more charitable than scientific," and himself takes a detached scientific approach to the battle, putting his efforts into the institution of new scientific public health projects such as the ones he has observed in France rather than into hands-on treatment of disease victims. These projects include the construction of the first local aqueduct, the first sewer system, and a covered public market, and they are no doubt of benefit to Urbino's fellow citizens. However, many of these projects also smack of the kind of self-promoting activities that might be undertaken by Flaubert's Homais, such as when the pharmacist encourages the disastrous surgery on poor Hippolyte not so much for the benefit of the club-foot as to prove the extent of his own enlightened knowledge.

Urbino's reliance on European models clearly participates in García Márquez' ongoing critique of the way in which Latin America has contributed to its own exploitation through its acceptance of the myth of foreign superiority. This link between Urbino and the imperialist domination of Latin America further clarifies the drive for power and dominance that is so central to Urbino's personality. At the death scene of Saint-Amour, Urbino speaks to the police inspector "as he would have to a subordinate," and indeed Urbino tends to treat everyone like subordinates, including his wife Fermina Daza. It is in his relationship with Fermina, in fact, that Urbino's style of relating to others through domination shows itself most clearly.

When he first begins his courtship of Fermina, Urbino does so very much in the manner of a military siege, and his early letters, though composed in an apparently "submissive spirit," already show an "impatience" that the independent-minded Fermina finds unsettling (124). And to press the courtship Urbino mobilizes whatever forces are at his command. Fermina's father Lorenzo, hungry for the social legitimation that would come to his daughter through a marriage to Urbino, eagerly encourages the courtship. Even more tellingly, Fermina has been expelled from her convent school for reading love letters from Florentino Ariza during class hours, and Urbino manages to induce the school to offer to reinstate Fermina if she will only entertain his advances.

Urbino's domineering style of courtship continues into the marriage, and despite certain indications early in the book that the Urbino–Daza marriage is nearly ideal, it becomes clear as the narrative progresses that the relationship is seriously flawed. Urbino's own rage for order and control can be seen in his unromantic proclamation that "the most important thing in a good marriage is not happiness, but stability" (300). Indeed, this practical attitude seems to form the very foundation of the marriage. Urbino marries Fermina though she is well below his social class, and he apparently does so because he believes that she will be a good and useful wife to him. As McNerney puts it, "She is a useful adornment, as befits the wife of a man like Urbino" (82).

But one suspects that Urbino marries below his social class at least partially because such a marriage gives him the leverage that he needs to feed his desire for dominance in the relationship. In any case, Fermina herself often feels trapped and constrained within a life that is clearly Urbino's more than hers. Late in the marriage she realizes that she is little more than a "deluxe servant" under Urbino's command:

> She always felt as if her life had been lent to her by her husband:
> she was absolute monarch of a vast empire of happiness, which
> had been built by him and for him alone. She knew that he loved
> her above all else, more than anyone else in the world, but only
> for his own sake: she was in his holy service. (221)

Indeed, Urbino is so overbearing that when he is forced to take a laxative he demands that his wife take one as well, so that she must share in his alimentary inconvenience (222).

That the private reality of the Urbino–Daza marriage is so different from the public perception of it is one of the strategies used by García Márquez in the book to indicate the seductiveness (and potential duplicity) of narrative. That the marriage is perfect makes a good story, and so the gullible townspeople generally accept that interpretation without question. But the construction of *Love*, in which the original presentation of the Urbino–Daza marriage is gradually undermined by the accumulation of additional details, makes the point that appearances can be deceiving and that one should not leap to interpretive conclusions hastily. This point is made most clearly by an interesting inconsistency in the narration of the book. Early on, when the marriage is still being presented as ideal, we are treated to a somewhat amusing anecdote from that marriage, in which Urbino's complaint that Fermina has failed to keep the bathroom stocked with soap mounts into a tempest-in-a-teapot crisis that is of course successfully resolved. And, we are told, this minor incident was the most critical problem that had ever arisen in the relationship: "When they recalled this episode, now they had rounded the corner of old age, neither could believe the astonishing truth that this had been the most serious argument in fifty years of living together" (29).

The very triviality of this argument reinforces the notion that the marriage is one without important difficulties. But there may be a good reason why "neither could believe" that this episode was their most serious marital problem. Late in the book we are suddenly told of Urbino's serious mid-life affair with the mulatta Bárbara Lynch, an affair of which Fermina learns and to which she reacts by moving out and going to live with her Cousin Hildebranda on her provincial ranch. Urbino finally convinces Fermina to return to him after a lengthy separation, but the incident has clearly posed a serious threat to the marriage. The jarring disjunction between the earlier account of the soap incident and this later story of Urbino's affair with Bárbara Lynch brings the reader to a sudden realization that the narrator of *Love* may not be entirely reliable and that we should be cautious about accepting anything we are told in the book at face value.

This emphasis on unreliable narration is reinforced at several points in the book, as when the newspaper *Justice* publishes (after Urbino's death) what is apparently an entirely fictitious account of an alleged love affair between Urbino and Fermina's friend Lucrecia del Real del Obispo. It may indeed be justice that this account is published, since the affair with Miss Lynch went undetected, but the fact that the quickly suppressed story finds believers (including Fermina herself) is a further warning against gullibility in reading. Of course, the most gullible reader of all in *Love* (and the most obvious link to Flaubert) is the hopeless *bovaryste* Florentino Ariza. Ariza's gullibility is established early in the book in his attempts to recover the treasure from a Spanish galleon that is rumored to have been sunk in the Caribbean just off the Colombian coast. Despite warnings that the attempt is folly, Ariza employs Euclides, a twelve-year-old boy, to dive for the treasure. Amazingly, the boy apparently finds the ship and begins to return with bits of jewelry supposedly recovered from the wreck. Ariza is about to mount a major salvage campaign when his mother (an experienced pawn broker) determines that the jewelry is fake and that Ariza has been duped by the boy.

Fermina treats the galleon episode as another example of Ariza's "poetic excesses," and it is true that Ariza is exceedingly susceptible to romantic fantasies in general. As with Emma Bovary, this susceptibility shows up most clearly in Ariza's reading of literature. The young Ariza devours the various volumes of the "Popular Library," a massive compilation of works that observes no distinctions of national origin or literary quality, including "everything from Homer to the least meritorious of the local poets" (75). At first glance, there is considerable potential in this compilation. From the point of view of Mikhail Bakhtin, one might find a source of carnivalesque energy in this conflation of "high" and "low" culture, a conflation that might potentially undermine the pretensions to seriousness and superiority of the European classics. Indeed, this combination of voices from official and from popular culture is reminiscent of the polyphonic intertextual voicing in García Márquez' own texts. But the point of the Bakhtinian carnival (or of the rich mixture of cultural voices in García Márquez) is to celebrate difference and diversity and to bring them out in the open. The totally indiscriminate compilation of the Popular Library, on the other hand, acts more to efface difference entirely, especially as it is read by Ariza, who "could not judge what was good and what was bad," knowing only that he prefers verse to prose, especially verse with predictable patterns of rhythm and rhyme that make it easy to memorize (75). The works in this library are mere commodities, all reduced to the same level of interchangeability.

Not only is Ariza an undiscriminating reader, but he is unduly influenced by what he reads, attempting to live his life in a way that is patterned after the poetry he reads. Thus, the poems he reads in the Popular Library became "the original source for his first letters to Fermina Daza, those half-baked endearments taken whole from the Spanish romantics" (75). Indeed, Ariza, though a poet of sorts, is so absorbed in the poetry of others that he is capable of writing only in the most imitative of fashions. When he employs his poetic skills to write love letters for others he writes not only in a style that mimics the poets he has read, but even in a handwriting that reproduces that of the supposed writers of the letter. And he is so successful in his imitations that lovers seek out his services to the point that he sometimes finds himself writing both sides of the communication and therefore producing entire simulated courtships.

Like Flaubert's Emma Bovary (and León Dupuis) Ariza identifies wholly with the books he reads, replacing the characters with real people he knows, "reserving for himself and Fermina Daza the roles of star-crossed lovers" (142). But despite this conflation of art and reality, Ariza uses poetry not to engage the world, but to escape from it. When he attempts to employ his skills as an imitator of styles to the writing of business letters, he fails completely. Throughout his career he suffers professionally because he is unable to write even the simplest business letter without ascending into an inappropriate lyricism. Even in matters of love Ariza's poetic bent can act as a wall between himself and reality, as when he immerses himself in love poetry in the midst of a "transient hotel" while remaining virtually oblivious to the activities of the prostitutes who surround him (75–76).

Fermina Daza provides a focal point at which Dr. Juvenal Urbino and Florentino Ariza converge, and there is an obvious element of dialogue between the science of Urbino and the poetry of Ariza that results from this convergence. But, as with the similar dialogue that occurs in *Madame Bovary* between Homais and Emma Bovary, this clash of discourses is highly complex. García Márquez, who depicts even the dictator in *Autumn of the Patriarch* with a sympathy that is often quite touching, shows his typical equanimity by presenting neither Urbino nor Ariza as entirely negative figures. Urbino's science does a great deal to improve the lot of the local populace, and Ariza's excessively romantic visions are in the end rewarded as he finally consummates his lifelong fascination with Fermina Daza. Still, Urbino's focus on science leads to a tunnel vision that cuts him off from genuinely human interactions and leads to his treatment of other people as objects for his own domination. And Ariza's absorption in poetry leads to a similar dehumanizing blindness, since he often treats others not as real people but as literary characters. For example, he seduces América Vicuña, a fourteen-year-old girl who has been entrusted to his guardianship, then summarily drops her when Urbino dies, making Fermina accessible to Ariza once again. The suggestively named América Vicuña then commits suicide, a victim of her own sheep-like gullibility and a symbol of the rape of Latin America by foreign powers.

Ariza's relationship with this girl is not that unusual in the fictional world of García Márquez, as the autumnal patriarch's fascination with young school girls amply illustrates. But Ariza's *bovarysme* invites comparison with literary models, and this particular autumn–spring relationship inevitably recalls that between Nabokov's Humbert Humbert and Lolita. Humbert, like Ariza, bears many similarities to Emma Bovary, and like Ariza his projection of his own aestheticized fantasies into the real world allows him to absorb other people within those fantasies, leaving them thoroughly objectified and "safely solipsized" (*Lolita* 62). Indeed, one suspects that Ariza has operated in this mode with all of the 622 "long-term liaisons" he has conducted during his "patient" wait for Fermina. Despite repeated suggestions in the text that Ariza has an unequalled capacity for love and that each of these 622 relationships is special and unique, enough is enough, and it seems clear on reflection that Ariza's initiation of new relationships at a clip of one per month for over fifty years bespeaks a lack of real emotional engagement in any of them. García Márquez' narrator describes a number of Ariza's affairs, apparently in an attempt to convince us of the sincerity and authenticity of Ariza's affections for his numerous conquests. And this attempt almost succeeds, despite the clear evidence that the affairs are simply too numerous for this sincerity to be possible. Narrative is a very seductive form, García Márquez seems to be telling us, and even the wisest of us must be on guard against gullibility in reading.[5]

The link to Nabokov helps to clarify this ongoing attack on gullibility. Humbert Humbert is a pervert, a rapist, and a murderer, and we are reminded repeatedly in *Lolita* of his mental and physical cruelty. Yet he is also a master of language who constructs a narrative so charming and so brilliant that many readers are seduced into sympathy with his position and are able to accept his claims that his relationship with Lolita was purely aesthetic. Similarly, Ariza's numerous love stories (especially the central one involving Fermina) make such attractive narratives that we are tempted to read him as the ideal lover he apparently thinks himself to be, not as a manipulative womanizer who jumps from one bed to another, causing considerable suffering and multiple violent deaths among the objects of this insatiable sexual appetite. Indeed, like Nabokov, García Márquez sprinkles his text with reminders of the sinister side of Ariza's sexual exploits—and exploitation. Perhaps the most telling of these concerns Olimpia Zuleta, a married woman whom he seduces after an extended siege. Afterwards, he marks his conquest by painting the woman's belly with the words "This pussy is mine" (217). That same night, her husband discovers the inscription and cuts her throat, whereupon Ariza's principal reaction is not remorse, but simply fear that the husband might discover his identity and come after him as well.

It is true, as most critics have realized, that the confrontation between Urbino and Ariza represents not just a competition between rivals in love, but also a clash of competing worldviews. Moraña seems to have understood this clash most fully:

> Vitalism and rationalism, modernization and tradition, Europeanization and popular culture, integration and marginality thus constitute poles in an ideological complex basically composed of Utopian projects that raise the question of the imposition of or resistance to foreign models. (40)

However, Moraña, like most other critics, goes on to conclude that *Love* privileges the romantic pole of this opposition, thereby offering a critique of the kind of modernization represented by Urbino. Yet the poet Ariza is just as domineering and manipulative as the scientist Urbino, and in many ways the two are not opposites but merely two sides of the same coin, just as Emma Bovary's love of literature is revealed by Flaubert to be a vulgar commodification of art that is merely the flipside of her insatiable materialism.

Both Ariza and Urbino make the same mistake—they accept the narratives that inform their lives without question, and this blind acceptance allows them to justify their lack of regard for others. And—like the patriarch, who becomes a prisoner of his own propaganda—both become the victims of their own narratives. Urbino fully accepts the standard nineteenth-century narrative of progress through scientific and technological advancement, and this acceptance not only blinds him to his own pompous and tyrannical attitudes but also to the destruction being wrought in South America by an unchecked and irresponsible development that is destroying natural resources such as the Magdalena River. Similarly, Ariza so fully accepts the narrative of the romantic lover that he cannot see the harm he is doing to others through his inveterate romancing.

Both Ariza and Urbino are, in short, gullible readers, and García Márquez' portrayal of them in *Love* constitutes a powerful indictment of such gullibility. But the book's most powerful statement on gullible reading occurs in the mechanics of the text itself, which seductively lures readers into reading it as a beautiful, poignant, and touching love story while ignoring the marry textual instabilities that so clearly undermine such a reading. As with his earlier use of magical realism in works such as *One Hundred Years of Solitude*, García Márquez demonstrates in *Love* that a well-told story can make readers accept almost anything. Despite the instances of unreliable narration in which the narrator seems to be caught in out and out lies, despite the radical disjunction between the content of the book and the romantic *follétin* form on which it is based, and despite the subversive Rabelaisian humor of the book, *Love* still makes for a terrific story.

García Márquez reinforces such readings in a number of ways, most obviously by constructing a story that most readers will *want* to read in a positive way, due to the undeniable affirmation of humanity contained in readings of the book that emphasize the romance of the Ariza–Daza relationship. Indeed, the consummation of this relationship after over fifty years of waiting can be read to offer a commentary on the nobility of the human spirit, and on one level the book clearly serves to affirm the validity of love and sexuality even in old age. Yet this apotheosis of romance is undermined by the text in a number of ways. For one thing, the entire culminating riverboat trip is shadowed by certain ominous notes, including the death of América Vicuña and the reported murder of another couple of aged lovers, also on a boat. Even the long-awaited climax of the courtship turns out to be an anti-climax. When the couple first goes to bed together, Ariza—the sexual adventurer *extraordinaire*—assures Fermina that he has remained a virgin throughout his life because of his devotion to her. Fermina does not believe this outrageous lie, because Ariza's "love letters were composed of similar phrases whose meaning mattered less than their brilliance" (339). Still, that such dishonesty is a standard feature of Ariza's discourse hardly makes it more excusable. Then, the first time the couple attempts to make love, Ariza is totally impotent, and he leaves Fermina's cabin in "martyrdom" (340). Later, when Ariza finally does make love to Fermina, he does so hastily and clumsily, completely without romance or regard for her feelings. She doesn't even have time to undress as he practically assaults her in a scene in which his penis is significantly described as a "weapon" being displayed as a "war trophy." Afterwards, we are told, Fermina "felt empty" (340).

Such scenes hardly support readings of *Love* as a celebration of septuagenarian sexuality, though it seems clear that the target of such episodes is not sex in old age, but overly romanticized notions of sexuality in general. One could also argue that the point of the Ariza–Daza relationship is not sex, but love, though the book tends to suggest that the two are not neatly separable. But even the romance of the ending, in which Ariza envisions Fermina and himself travelling endlessly up and down the Magdalena River, is seriously undermined by other elements of the narrative.[6] In particular, the river has been ravaged by industrialization and "progress," and has become virtually unnavigable. Ariza's final fantasy of endlessly cruising the river, like most of his fantasies, is an impossible one that fails to take reality into account, and perhaps the message is that such unrealistic romantic visions have themselves contributed to the demise of the river by blinding the local populace to what is really going on in their country.

One of the most striking features of *Love* is that it can remain so seductive as a story of romance in spite of the way in which the text continually self-destructs as a romantic narrative. Much of this effect can be attributed to García Márquez' brilliance as a storyteller, of course, but much of it has to do with the nature of the narrative itself. *Love* very clearly suggests a complicity between the desire of Florentino Ariza for Fermina Daza and the reader's desire for a successful consummation of the text. But the book works its seductive magic in other ways as well, some of which are highly significant as aspects of the ongoing attack on gullible reading. One of the more interesting techniques employed in the book is the frequent use of real historical personages and events, whose appearance in the text tends to create an air of verisimilitude. When we read that Jeremiah de Saint-Amour has played chess with Capablanca (32), or that Juvenal Urbino studied with the father of Marcel Proust (114), or that Fermina Daza was chosen to greet Charles Lindbergh when he visited Colombia (306), there is a tendency for the entire plot to seem more realistic. Similarly, one of the reasons that Ariza is so easily duped by the boy Euclides in the episode of the Spanish galleon is that the story of the sunken ship is made more believable by the existence of specific historical information. For example, Ariza finds records which indicate that a fleet of ships led by the flagship San José had arrived in Colombia from Panama in May 1708, and is even able to find documentation concerning the number of ships, their exact route, and the circumstances under which they were sunk (90–91).

Yet there is also evidence that the entire story of the sunken ships was fabricated by a dishonest viceroy in an effort to hide his own thefts from the Spanish Crown (93). Likewise, *Love* is pure fiction, and a careful inspection shows that many of the concrete historical details in the book are impossible, anachronistic, or simply fictionalized. In short, history can be faked, and the reader who unquestioningly accepts official narratives of historical events is liable to be just as deceived as is Florentino Ariza in his reading of bad romantic poetry. Indeed, *Love* is principally a book not about romance, but about history and politics. Totalitarianism and imperialism thrive on the blind acceptance of their official narratives, and the gullible reading of these narratives by an unsuspecting populace makes their domination all the easier. The saccharine surface of *Love in the Time of Cholera* conceals a series of diabolical textual traps in a dynamic of duplicity very similar to that so familiar to victims of domination and dictatorship everywhere. García Márquez presents a narrative so seductive as to be almost irresistible, yet so complex as to be largely lost on those who fall prey to its seduction. The message is clear: even the best readers (and the most alert citizens) are ever in danger of being duped by a good story, whether that story be contained in a book of fiction or in the proclamations of a tyrant.

NOTES

1. Paul de Man's update of the Marx Aveling English translation of this passage reads "having at the time of the cholera distinguished myself by a boundless devotion" (253). The translation is quite literal, Flaubert's original French reading "s'être, lors du choléra, signalé par un dévouement sans borne" (408).

2. García Márquez' title presumably refers to the fact that the aged lovers Florentino

Ariza and Fermina Daza end the book, together at last, sailing endlessly up and down the Great Magdalena River on a riverboat which flies a cholera flag to discourage other passengers from coming aboard. There is a secondary resonance in the title which indicates the way that love sometimes endures despite negative developments (such as cholera epidemics) in the world around it. But the incongruous juxtaposition of "love" and "cholera" in the title also functions as a hint that the book's love story may not be quite what it appears.

3. On this aspect of *One Hundred Years of Solitude* see Connif.

4. Note, for example, his enthusiasm over the impetus given to his career in recent years through a switch to a personal computer for the composition of his texts (Williams 134).

5. It is, of course, quite possible that the unreliable narrator of *Love* has himself exaggerated the number of Ariza's affairs.

6. See Fiddian for a further discussion of the ambiguity of this ending (198).

WORKS CITED

Bell-Villada, Gene H. *García Márquez: The Man and His Work*. Chapel Hill: U of North Carolina P, 1990.

Conniff, Brian. "The Dark Side of Magical Realism: Science, Oppression, and Apocalypse in *One Hundred Years of Solitude*." *Modern Fiction Studies* 36 (Summer 1990): 167–79.

Fiddian, Robin. "A Prospective Post-Script: Apropos of *Love in the Times of Cholera*." In *Gabriel García Márquez: New Readings*. Ed. Bernard McGuirk and Richard Cardwell. Cambridge: Cambridge UP, 1987. 191–20

Flaubert, Gustave. *Madame Bovary*. Lausanne: Éditions Rencontre, 1965.

———. *Madame Bovary*. Trans. Paul de Man based on the translation by Eleanor Marx Aveling. New York: W.W. Norton, 1965.

García Márquez, Gabriel. *Love in the Time of Cholera*. Trans. Edith Grossman. New York: Penguin, 1989.

Horkheimer, Max and Theodor W. Adorno. *Dialectic of Enlightenment*. Trans. John Cumming. New York: Seabury P, 1972.

Janes, Regina. *Gabriel García Márquez: Revolutions in Wonderland*. Columbia: U of Missouri P, 1981.

McNerney, Kathleen. *Understanding Gabriel García Márquez*. Columbia: U of South Carolina P, 1989.

Moraña, Mabel. "Modernity and Marginality in *Love in the Time of Cholera*." *Studies in Twentieth–Century Literature* 14 (Winter 1990): 27–43.

Nabokov, Vladimir. *The Annotated Lolita*. Ed. Alfred Appel, Jr. New York and Toronto: McGraw-Hill, 1970.

Williams, Raymond Leslie. "The Visual Arts, the Poeticization of Space and Writing: An Interview with Gabriel García Márquez." *PMLA* 104 (1989): 131–40.

ANNY BROOKSBANK JONES

Utopia and Other Commonplaces in García Márquez's El Amor en Los Tiempos del Cólera

A number of critics have noted what Verity Smith calls García Márquez's 'growing concern with the position of women in society' and the shifts in their characterization since *Cien años de soledad* (1967).[1] For Sandra Maria Boschetto this process begins with *Crónica de una muerte anunciada* (1981), in which 'García Márquez undertakes [...] a view of women in which, although granted that the outline is more sketchy, the figure is more convincing'.[2] Later in the same article Boschetto nevertheless admits to being disturbed by certain episodes in *Crónica*, for example when Angela Vicario 'falls madly in love' on her wedding night 'with the man who rejects her like a dirty rag' (p. 130). Apart from a closing observation to the effect that García Márquez fares rather better when he is dealing with art than with life—a more problematic distinction in this context that she acknowledges—Boschetto does not attempt to bring these two observations together.

What follows is an exploration of the tension that Boschetto (half) observes, based on the novel published four years after *Crónica*, *El amor en los tiempos del cólera*.[3] Reading such tension as symptomatic of the negotiations demanded of each of us as relations between men and women continue to change, the article explores the place of stereotypes in this process, and closes with some thoughts on García Márquez's own much-debated relation to his feminist readers.

From *The Modern Language Review* 89, Part 3 (July 1994). © 1994 Modern Humanities Research Association.

According to the dustjacket of the Bruguera edition, *El amor* sets before the reader 'una suerte de inventario pasional que consigna tanto las crudas imposiciones de la carne como los meandros sutiles del sentimiento porque "el corazón tiene más cuartos que un hotel de putas", y porque el amor es un fluido que se expande como los círculos tejidos por una piedra en un estanque'.[4] The dustjacket also highlights the novel's use of 'los ingredientes clásicos del género folletinesco'. In an interview published four years later, however, García Márquez emphasizes a rather different source: 'In reality it's my parents' love story. I heard my father and mother both talk about these love stories. That's why the story is set during the period of their youth, although I put much of the story back even further in time. My father was a telegrapher who also played the violin and wrote love poems' (Williams, p. 138).

As is so often the case, the exact status of correlations and divergences between García Márquez's 'facts' and his 'fiction' is questionable. I am talking not about his parents' relationship or their love but about their 'love story'—a representation that is already inextricable from talk about (other/s') 'love stories'. Events and details from his parents' marriage and his own marriage may figure in those of his characters, but García Márquez is quite clear that Florentino's concept of love is 'totally ideal and [...] doesn't correspond to reality'; it owes more to 'bad poetry' (Williams, p. 131).[5] In an author who holds that 'you can only get to good poetry by means of bad poetry' one would expect 'bad' to be a rather flexible term, and a number of *El amor*'s critics have indeed noted that stereotypes from sentimental poetry and popular literature are represented in the novel with considerable sympathy, nostalgia, and attention to detail.[6] Michael Wood and Stephen Minta take this further: for Minta 'the novel deals confidently in cliché and improbable exaggeration, searching for truths about emotional life which, the book implies, are as solidly embedded in the language of the popular imagination as in the most subtle language of psychological analysis'.[7] Wood, however, is unconvinced by the power of such stereotypes to reveal truths, and suggests that García Márquez's fondness for the clichés he deploys is so evident as to undermine or leave little room for irony in their representation:

> The novel is not an old-fashioned serial but [...] it isn't far enough away for irony. [...] If he moves away from his stereotypes, he begins to condescend to them, and to drop their truths for his. If he repeats them, he can only gesture vaguely, as they do, towards those complex truths—can hint that they are there, but not focus on them with any precision.[8]

The implications of Minta's and Wood's assumptions become clear when they are referred to specific stereotypical encounters in the novel. One particularly striking example is Florentino Ariza's affair with Sara Noriega. Although she, too, fails to win a prize at the 'Juegos Florales' her disappointment and 'aflicción sincera' are reserved exclusively for him (p. 286). Back at her chambers, one kiss from Florentino is enough to bend her entire body, 'monumental, ávido y cálido' to his will (p. 286). The climax of the encounter is more like a transfiguration, as the maternal eroticism of her 'tetamenta astronómica' is displaced by the 'chupón de niño' which Sara 'tenía que succionar [...] para alcanzar la gloria plena' (p. 289).

Among the less attractive features of the encounter is some excruciating feline claw-play, when Florentino 'tuvo que resignarse a tener en la cama al gato enfurecido' of his lover (p. 291). Sara's 'gato' is only one of the alien elements in this particular encounter. She is as knowledgeable and as available as fantasy requires because she was consigned by her first boyfriend to 'un limbo de novia burlada' and left with an illegitimate child (p. 289). This glimmer of social realism is quickly subordinated to erotic fancy: the experience 'no la dejó ninguna amargura' and she continues to believe that 'no valía la pena vivir si no era para tener un hombre en la cama' (p. 289). Minta may well be right when he observes that the novel 'constantly challenges the reader to adopt a knowing, cynical, or sophisticated response to the events described, and then works hard to ensure victory for a certain kind of innocence' (p. 128). The success of this hard work is, however, finally indistinguishable from the failure of distance suggested by Wood: in both cases the reader is confronted with highly dubious but lovingly depicted stereotypical features and no focused or sustained point from which they might be seriously questioned.

Boschetto offers a slightly different perspective on García Márquez's failures and successes when she notes that what is a failure in *Crónica* at one level ('the world'), may be a triumph at another ('art') (p. 134). The difficulties of this type of distinction, particularly in relation to *El amor*, have already been suggested; more interesting in this context is the tension that leads Boschetto to posit it. As noted, this tension arises between García Márquez's increasingly detailed and complex female characters and his continuing use from time to time of clichéd encounters between men and women which seem to have very little to redeem them in feminist—and arguably in human—terms. One striking example concerns the 'negra, joven y bonita' Leona Cassiani, for example, who having been left 'tirada sobre las piedras, llena de cortaduras por todo el cuerpe' after a violent rape, spends the rest of her life seeking out the perpetrator for more of his good, hard 'amor' (p. 376).

We cannot simply blame these unreconstructed moments on García Márquez's popular sources and maintain that his own larger vision overrides them: first, because, as noted, the balance does seem to remain largely in favour of popular sources, and second, because the distinction between unreconstructed and reconstructed moments is, in practice, rarely clear cut. Take, for example, the case of Lotario Thugut, 'que se daba una vida de rey explotando a tres mujeres al mismo tiempo. Las tres le rendían cuentas al amanecer, humilladas a sus pies para hacerse perdonar sus recaudos exiguos, y la única gratificación que anhelaban era que él se acostara con la que llevaba más dinero' (p. 100).

Having confronted the all too familiar image of exploited and humiliated women with his usual gusto, García Márquez does gesture towards a question. The character's name goes some way to refraining the encounter, and there is a suggestion of further refraining when Florentino speculates that 'sólo el terror podía inducir a semejante indignidad' (p. 100). Now if (and only if) Nancy Friday and her disciples are to be believed, erotic fantasies (even feminists' erotic fantasies) bristle with such imagined indignities, any of which would be unthinkable outside their fantasy setting. When García Márquez confronts erotic fantasy with 'indignidad' and 'terror', there is a brief, jarring recognition of this incoherence. It is smoothed over instantly, however, when one of the women explains that 'estas cosas [...] sólo pueden hacerse por amor' (p. lot).

This could be read as a victory for Minta's 'certain kind of innocence', recidivism, or something else. After all, there may indeed be something to be said for reuniting love and the erotic, so often sundered in certain types of contemporary fiction. That is not the same thing as conflating them, however. Gene Bell-Villada notes:

> As has often been commented, there is almost every possible sort of male–female tie in *Love*—older-younger affair and vice versa, female-on-male rape and vice versa, adultery and masturbation, prostitution, jilting, crime of passion, suicide for love, conjugal affection, unconsummated sexual attraction, young love, elderly love, and a formal courtship complete with chaperone and go-between. (p. 194)[9]

Yet though this inventorial approach seems to exhaust all options, some—most notably the western liberal ideal of an exclusive, enduring, reciprocal, and symmetrically powered (heterosexual or homosexual) relation—do not figure at all, while others receive disproportionate attention. The reader is reminded more than once, for example, that 'se puede estar enamorado de varias personas a la vez [...] sin traicionar a ninguna' because 'el corazón tiene más cuartos que un hotel de putas' (p. 394). Simply insisting on variety does not guarantee polyvalence, however: the novel's dustjacket confirms that the same sort of thing is happening in every single 'cuarto' by reducing all options to either 'los meandros sutiles del sentimiento' or 'las crudas imposiciones de la carne'. Although Fermina is arguably the only recipient of the first kind of 'amor', her most virulent detractor (Sara Noriega) restricts even this to something like a subset of the second kind, when she divides love into 'amor del alma de la cintura para arriba y amor del cuerpo de la cintura para abajo' (p. 292).

What does tend to unite the head and the body, while further restricting options for the novel's women characters, is the fact that sentimental and fleshly impositions have key features in common. Of these perhaps the most obvious is the gaze with which—chronic myopia (or eyestrain) notwithstanding—Florentino fixes his objects.[10] At one end of the spectrum are the shy or sly glances reserved for Fermina; at the other is the what-the-butler-saw, *grand guignol* type of encounter reserved for Sara Noriega and others. Of course, Florentino himself is not much to look at: 'Era escúalido [...] con un cabello indio sometido con pomada de olor, y los espejuelos de miope que aumentaban su aspecto de desamparo. Aparte del defecto de la vista, sufría de un estreñimiento crónico que lo obligó a aplicarse lavativas purgantes toda la vida' (pp. 86–87). This apparent 'defecto de la vista' helps to augment his appeal to women: 'A pesar de su aire desmirriado, de su retraimiento y de su vestimenta sombría, las muchachas de su grupo hacían rifas secretas para jugar a quedarse con él' (pp. 86–87). Attempts to extend his vision—in the local lighthouse, for example, where 'aprendió a alimentar la luz [...] a dirigirla y a aumentarla con espejos' (p. 144)—are finally unsatisfying, and when he uses the 'catalejo' installed up there to survey 'las playas de mujeres' below, 'no podía verse más ni nada más excitante de lo que podía verse en la calle' (p. 145).

Without these aids, however, Florentino finds love everywhere he looks. Even Fermina Daza's resistance is finally worn down, apparently by his conviction that the most striking and difficult of women will succumb to the most unprepossessing man if he needs her enough. Throughout this time Florentino's gaze sustains a sentimental attachment that has almost no reciprocal dimension, either verbal or physical. The initial 'cataclismo de amor' is triggered by a casual glance—the glance, it seems, of a girl who 'levantó la vista para ver quién pasaba por la ventan' (p. 88). Nothing is said about the perceiver of that look, though Florentino will himself have needed rather more than a glance to interpret the 'visión rara' of a girl teaching her aunt to read, and to recognize his ideal love object (p. 88). He pursues her obsessively: at first 'con ver a la niña le bastaba' but 'poco a poco fue idealizándola' until, by his efforts, she becomes a 'doncella', transfigured and fixed 'con la alquimia de la poesía' (pp. 90, 101).

Others, meanwhile, are constructing Fermina rather differently. Like Florentino, 'la tía Escolástica' monitors her niece's every move and does not leave him 'el menor resquicio para acercarse' (p. 90). Like the riverboat captain in the novel's closing pages, however, she is won over by Florentino's ability to speak as if 'por inspiración del Espíritu Santo' (p. 104). The nuns who watch Fermina in the name of her father are more hard-headed, forcing Florentino to appeal to Lorenzo Daza directly. This time, even 'el Espíritu Santo' cannot help him: Daza sends his daughter away 'aquella misma mañana [...] al viaje del olvido' (p. 127).

Catching sight of the mature Fermina on her return home Florentino 'se sintió sacudido por un estremecimiento sísmico' (p. 150): 'La espiaba', 'en estado natural'; 'la perseguía sin aliento', 'sin dejarse ver' (pp. 151–53). When Fermina finally intercepts his gaze, 'despertó del hechizo. [...] En un instante se le reveló completa la magnitud de su propio engaño' (p. 155). Years later, when Fermina is still refusing to see him, Florentino watches her reflection in a restaurant mirror and buys it 'no por los primores del marco, sino por el espacio interior, que había sido ocupado durante dos horas por la imagen amada' (p. 334). As he scans it for a glimpse of his love the mirror does not crack, and nor does the novelistic world. Not until she finally responds to his solicitations will he see Fermina's image in the glass. Until then the reader cannot even be sure he sees his own, for with the help of Fermina and his supplementary loves, Florentino is 'todo amor' (p. 193): without it he is a slightly sinister 'necesitado de amor' (p. 226) who, like Fantomas, Mr Hyde, or Cortázar's Laurent, hunts, 'pajaritas' by night (p. 256), and is notable chiefly for 'his shadowy unreality, his apparent nothingness'.[11]

This preference for illicit watching leads Florentino to exercise custody of the eyes in the one place where 'ver y dejarse ver' are actively promoted as 'refinamientos de príncipes en Europa' and accommodated in 'cubiculos de cartón con agujeros de alfileres, que lo mismo se alquilaban para hacer que para ver' (p. 100). In the local bordello it is, perversely, 'la lectura' (p. 116) in a room reserved for the purpose that is his 'vicio insaciable' (p. 101). He also discovered 'los secretos del amor sin amor', though it has to be said that accounts of his initiation—the fully dressed male revelling in a 'paraíso de la desnudez [femenina]', for example—are rooted in equally familiar fantasies (p. 118). One particularly striking encounter involves a woman whose marginal character echoes his own. The 'encargada de la limpieza' is 'joven' but 'envejecida'; dressed like a 'penitente en la gloria de la desnudez' she collects 'preservativos usados' and other refuse of 'amor' (p. 120). He sees her 'a diario sin sentirse visto', until one day she mistakes his own preserved love for leftovers and tries to lay hands on it: 'pasó cerca de la cama y él sintió la mano tibia y tierna', fetishistically severed from the desiring body, 'en la cruz de su vientre', 'la sintió buscándolo, la sintió encontrarlo, la sintió soltándole los botones' (p. 120). This is perhaps another familiar fantasy, but this time with no climax; for the moment at least Florentino has eyes only for Fermina. He nevertheless pretends to read until his own desire becomes strikingly visible and 'tuvo que esquivar el cuerpo' (p. 120). By keeping his mind (half) on the sentimental pleasures of fidelity he can enjoy the woman's bodily desire without returning it, and in the process have his own desirability affirmed. This initiation prefigures all Florentino's subsequent affairs: in Fermina's case he is described as cultivating his obsession until her husband is dead; in all other cases it is the image of Fermina and the act of cultivation that distract him.

Later, having decided to preserve only sentimental love for Fermina, Florentino can indulge his 'ojo certero para conocer de inmediato a la mujer que lo esperaba, así fuera en medio de una muchedumbre' (pp. 225–26). There appears to be no shortage of takers: Josefa Zúñiga is 'loca de amor por él'; Prudencia Pitre 'le habría vendido el alma al diablo por casarse con él'; Sara Noriega 'abandonaba lo que estuviera haciendo, fuera lo que fuera, y se consagraba el cuerpo entero a tratar de hacerlo feliz' (pp. 393, 416, 290). And this is all because 'lo identificaban de inmediato como [...] un menesteroso de la calle con una humildad de perro apaleado que las rendía sin condiciones, sin pedir nada, sin esperar nada de él, aparte de la tranquilidad de conciencia de haberle hecho el favor' (p. 226).

At first glance this arrangement looks satisfactory for all concerned: a certain absence of qualities means that Florentino has nothing women can demand of him, while boundless compassion on their part ensures that they would not want it if he had. 'Menesterosas' like the 'encargada de la limpieza' will be disappointed, but this need not stop them playing their part alongside Florentino's other women, helping him to forget his ideal love, and to prove that he cannot forget her. In the process these supplementary 'amores' punish Fermina, yet they give Florentino the self-confidence to aspire to her; they keep him fit and sexually active for her; they help him accept the aging process and their aging competitor as a sexual partner; they bring him a certain status and wealth to pass on to her when the moment of union comes.

The (seemingly paradoxical) notion that women construct their self-image in the selfless service of others is distinctly unpromising for women who are not so inclined, and even, it could be argued, for those who are. This novel's version of it—that women find dependency in men attractive and derive their own pleasure from engaging with it—is potentially less objectionable, particularly when it is linked with a principal character who depends explicitly on women for his own sense of self. Once again, however, the narrative model he has chosen prevents García Márquez from developing the potential he registers. By the time Florentino is in a position to take the hand of the strong-willed woman who rejected him for his weakness, the narrative-drive towards consummation is flattening all other stories and possibilities. When Florentino reflects that 'había hecho y pensado todo lo que había hecho en la vida, llegaba a la cumbre sin otra causa que la determinación encarnizada de estar vivo y en buen estado de salud en el momento de asumir su destino' (p. 391) he makes no mention of the team pulling him from above. Indeed, 'seiscientos veintidós [...] amores continuados' after their first meeting he tells Fermina: 'sin un temblor en la voz: Es que me he conservado virgen para ti' (p. 490).

At first sight her lover's lifelong habit of duplicity and non-reciprocity make the prognosis for Fermina less than promising. Yet if, as the narrative sometimes suggests, adventures of 'sentimiento' and 'carne' are generically incommensurable and thus discontinuous, there is a sense in which he is not lying when he says he has remained a virgin for her. It would be rather easier to sustain this line, however, if his lists of conquests did not include fleshly attachments that were also romantic: there is the dazzling Angeles Alfaro, 'la efímera y la más amada de todas' (p. 393); there is the affair with Olimpia Zuleta, 'la única vez, desde los primeros tiempos del primer amor en que sintió atravesado por una lanza' (p. 317); there is 'la viuda de Nazaret', 'la única que irradiaba ternura de sobra como para sustituir a Fermina' (p. 392). With the widow in particular, the distance between Fermina and her rival, sentiment and body, has narrowed almost to nothing, and must be reaffirmed by other means: 'lograron ser amantes intermitentes durante casi treinta años gracias a su divisa de mosqueteros: *Infieles, pero no desleales*' (p. 393). Since 'desleal', according to the *Vox Diccionario General de la Lengua Española*, signifies 'que no guarda la debida fidelidad' and 'infiel' may be defined as 'falto de fidelidad' this reaffirmation is less persuasive than it seems. It is further undermined by Florentino's reaction to the death of Olimpia Zuleta: hearing that his lover's throat has been cut by her husband, 'no le temía tanta la navaja en el cuello, ni el escándalo público, como a la mala suerte de que Fermina se enterara de su deslealtad' (p. 318). It seems that the narrative, itself wilfully 'infiel' or 'falto de exactitud', is once again positing distinctions it cannot sustain.

I have already made some observations concerning Florentino's supplementary relations, but before I examine the effects of these clashing disloyalties in the novel's closing pages, something needs to be said about Fermina's own past loves. There is little evidence of romance in her marriage to Dr Juvenal Urbino, though it appears to bring her all the economic security, social power, and respectability her disreputable father had hoped for. Minta describes this marriage as:

> A world of happiness from which there is no escape, in which she has largely ceased to exist except as the source of happiness and security for another, her husband's shield against the terrors of life and death. It is a relationship that has found its best moments in a carefully contrived harmony of apparently mutual support, but it has never quite passed beyond that. (p. 140)

For Minta, Urbino is the novel's principal character, 'the centre of authority against which the book so joyously rebels' (p. 140). Given Fermina's economic dependence, however, rebellion against domestic attrition and her husband's infidelity is available to her only in a very limited form. It is not clear what happiness for an independent-minded woman might be in these circumstances, but describing their relationship as one of 'apparently mutual support' is rather like tying someone's legs to a tree and calling it a crutch. For all this, the detailed accounts of social and domestic irritations, the small joys and larger incomprehensions, suggest that the novel's model of married love is the 'middle' of the story, for which García Márquez turned from his parents' 'love stories' to his own 'life'.[12] For all its shortcomings, there is a sense in which infatuation sustained by sentimental fantasy and non-consummation is hardly more attractive, yet almost as soon as her husband is off the scene Florentino inherits 'el amor que se le había quedado sin dueño' (p. 476).

Fermina is eased through this transition by the supplement to Florentino's *Secretario de los enamorados*, which contains the insights of a lifetime, 'con base en sus ideas y experiencias de las relaciones entre hombre y mujer' (p. 425). The status of these 'relations' has already been questioned and is highlighted in the novel's closing pages in a way which suggests that women who restrict their aspirations to crudely imposed flesh may be lucky to get even that. When Florentino fails to achieve an erection during the long-awaited union with Fermina, the Barcelona first edition states that 'le ocurrió siempre la primera vez, con todas, desde siempre' (p. 491). This goes some way to explaining the exclusion of one-night stands from his twenty-five little black books. But the effect of Florentino's admission on less understanding readers is modified in the Penguin translation of the first Colombian edition, and simply observes that 'it had happened to him sometimes'.[13] In both accounts another telling mismatch precedes (and is presumably implicated in) this non-consummation. Gazing for the first time on her nakedness, Florentino notes Fermina's 'hombros arrugados, los senos caidos y el costillar forrado de un pellejo pálido y frio como el de una rana' (p. 490). He, on the other hand, appears before her as 'un hombre sin edad, de piel oscura, lúcida y tensa como un paraguas abierto [...] que no se dejaba ver el arma por casualidad, sino que la exhibía como un trofeo de guerra' (p. 492).

Fermina has exchanged a life in which 'lo más importante [no era] la felicidad sino la estabilidad' (p. 435) for one in which 'el amor [era] un origin y un fin en sí mismo' (p. 425), in which the unprepossessing young man she had rejected is himself transfigured by love. She, however, is not. What is heralded as an affirmation of love in old age looks increasingly like the substitution of one fantasy for another, another case of 'deslealtad'. Fermina takes her place in his fantasy no longer as idealized love, nor yet as equal partner, but as an elderly, surrogate wife. Since he need now look no further, she wears his spectacles to sew buttons on his shirt, becomes as it were his pupil, and learns to see things his way. The vanishing-point of the seer and the seen is represented as 'más allá de las burlas brutales de las ilusiones y los espejismos de los desengaños: más allá del amor' (p. 499) or, as the Penguin translation puts it, at the very 'heart of love' (p. 345). The voice of her lover is once again 'iluminada por la gracia del Espiritu Santo', while the boat's captain speaks as 'el destino' (p.502). Yet while 'destino' looks in awe on Florentino's 'dominio invencible, su amor impávido', when the captain glances in Fermina's direction he sees on an old lady's eyelashes 'los primeros destellos de escarcha invernal' (p. 348).

Once the radical disjunction between Florentino and Fermina is evident to third parties, it can no longer be attributed to her assumption of his idealizing gaze. Instead, her depreciation seems to represent the continuing possibility of irony, a reminder that even if a place beyond illusion is itself inaccessible to irony one can nevertheless be deluded about being there.

In my earlier discussion of irony and cliché Michael Wood was cited to the effect that García Márquez can gesture towards stereotypes' complex truths 'but not focus on them with any precision'. There are alternatives to Wood's implied deficit model, however, and they include the possibility that there are nothing but stereotypes to describe existing relations between men and women. Wood and Minta both assume that there are truths behind stereotypes which García Márquez may or may not be able to retrieve. For Luce Irigaray, the most subtle of so-called utopian feminists, it is not a question of revealing, so much as producing truths there. In her view, the repertoire of socially sanctioned representations of relations between men and women is a limited one and heavily dependent on stereotype. Since it nevertheless offers the only terms in which we can talk about these relations *and be understood*, Irigaray proposes that we assume these terms and hollow them out, as it were, from within to make room for new possibilities. As Rosi Braidotti notes, Irigaray's exploitation of stereotypes, this 'apparent mimesis', is 'tactical and aims at *producing* difference'.[14] It is possible to trace something like a tactical mimesis in *El amor*, a half-ironic dramatization of the conflict between a yearning for the familiar and a desire to make something new of the old, jaded terms. Florentino's relationship with Ausencia Santander, the apotheosis of incomprehensible ('sin-entender') absence, seems to typify this process. At nearly fifty, Ausencia has 'un instinto tan personal para el amor, que no había teorías artesanales ni científicas capaces de entorpecerlo' (p. 260). She strips off Florentino's clothes as soon as he puts his head round the door:

> Lo asaltaba sin darle tiempo de nada, ya fuera en el mismo sofá donde acababa de desnudarlo [...]. Se le metía debajo y se apoderaba de todo él para ella, encerrada dentro de sí misma, tanteando con los ojos cerrados en su absoluta oscuridad interior, avanzando por aquí, retrocediendo, corrigiendo su rumbo invisible, intentando otra vía más intensa, otra forma de andar sin naufragar en la marisma de mucílago que fluía de su vientre, preguntándose y contestándose a sí misma con un zumbido de moscardón en su jerga nativa dónde estaba ese algo en las tinieblas que sólo ella conocía y ansiaba sólo para ella, hasta que sucumbía sin esperar a nadie, se desbarrancaba sola en su abismo con una explosión jubilosa de victoria total que hacía temblar el mundo. (pp. 261–62)

Florentino, however, 'se quedaba exhausto, incompleto, flotando en el charco de sudores de ambos, pero con la impresión de no ser más que un, instrumento de gozo' (p. 262).

This is, arguably, the text's only example of a self-seeking woman, and its only suggestion that there is 'algo', an 'absoluta oscuridad', in certain women at least, that is inaccessible to Florentino. Readers may, however, recognize in this 'algo' and in his response to it, echoes of Nietzsche and Freud on the narcissistic woman. As Florentino contemplates the abyss of women's sexuality he thinks he glimpses in all its terrible fascination the form of a dark continent, or the black hole that declares the absence of the phallus. Framed by this exquisite anxiety, 'amor ensimismado' becomes 'una trampa de la felicidad que él aborrecía y anhelaba al mismo tiempo' (p. 262).

These words signal the risks involved in remotivating old terms.

Florentino's mixed loathing and longing are stirred by the possibility of 'ese algo' irreducible to existing models. Yet when a stereotype is hollowed out to suggest an 'oscuridad interior'—the space left, for example, when an old representation is abandoned—it can instantly be refilled by speculation on the old (male) fear of and desire of self-loss (p. 262). As long as Ausencia figures exclusively as the object of Florentino's reflections, the possibility of a non-stereotypical representation of her desire remains secondary to his concerns about that possibility, and about the possibility of losing the marker of his own desire.

The affair with Ausencia Santander allows the reader to explore certain apparently more promising aspects of the stereotype, but it is neither female desire nor male that concerns me here so much as the changing relations between them. This article began with the negotiations that these changes demand, and cited the novel's dustjacket to the effect that 'el amor es un fluido que se expande como los círculos tejidos por una piedra en un estanque'. It closes with another watery metaphor, negotiated relations, and their place in the novel's ending.

Something has already been said about the vision of Fermina as an aging but indispensable object of transcendental love in an unending vista of semi-domestic concubinage. Florentino could not marry her even if he wanted to, because the only models on offer are the unfaithful wife/vengeful husband, or the straitjacket of official love. Like the captain of the riverboat, Florentino 'no encontraba cómo salir del embrollo en que se había metido' (p. 502). This moment, when stereotypes are finally exhausted, appears as the culmination of their—or his—love story: 'sigamos derecho', Florentino orders the captain, 'derecho, derecho' (p. 502). Readers less inclined to give García Márquez the benefit of the doubt may read this as the point at which the retreat from contemporary turmoil to fantasies of 'amor inquebrantable' finally runs out of river, and is left endlessly repeating itself. Among more sympathetic readings is one in which 'el amor' is left to expand, while the novel waits in watery suspense until an alternative ending can be found, one that requires neither domestic drudgery nor exploitation, nor escapist fantasy, 'más allá del amor' in its existing forms. Until then (and, no doubt, even then) the old stereotypes will remain in evidence as the ground against which changes are registered.

Whether or not one subscribes to this view of the novel's radical possibilities it would be a pity to overlook the more direct appeal of *El amor*. There will be those who prefer to leave García Márquez to his ducks and drakes and other more or less innocent pleasures; and there will be others who opt to follow the text's example, indulge themselves, and exploit any utopian or other possibilities as they seem to arise. Given the complexity and inconsistencies of *El amor*, the choice made will depend more on our own critical and personal priorities than on García Márquez's supposed 'feminism' or otherwise.

NOTES

1. Review of Kathleen McNerney's *Understanding Gabriel García Márquez*, *MLR*, 85 (1990), 774–75 (p. 775).

2. 'The Demythication of Matriarchy and Image of Women in *Chronicle of a Death Foretold*', in *Critical Perspectives on Gabriel García Márquez*, ed. by B.A. Shaw and N. Vera-Godwin (Lincoln, NB: Society of Spanish and Spanish-American Studies, 1986), pp. 125–37 (p. 125). The novel is hereafter referred to as '*Crónica*'.

3. (Barcelona: Bruguera, 1985), hereafter referred to as *El amor*. All further textual references are to this edition.

4. As the author confirms in Raymond Leslie Williams, 'The Visual Arts, the Poetization of Space and Writing: An Interview with Gabriel García Márquez', *PMLA*, 104 (1989), 131–40 (p. 136), the setting is modelled on Cartagena, Colombia, with occasional additions (such as the Café de la Parroquia) from Veracruz and elsewhere. Significantly, in this context, he recalls the time spent in Cartagena as 'the best year of my life, the most mature [in] the sense of feeling an absolute emotional stability' (p. 137).

5. Consider also: 'When I saw how, past the age of seventy, [my parents] were still sweethearts, I was sure they would make a good novel [...]. The big problem was the middle, but life teaches you about the centre of things' (interview with Holly Aylett, 'Of Love and Levitation', in *Times Literary Supplement*, 4516, October, 1989, pp. 1152, 65 (p. 1152)).

6. See, for example, Gene Bell-Villada, *García Márquez: The Man and His Work* (Chapel Hill: University of North Carolina Press, 1990), pp. 191–202.

7. Stephen Minta, *Gabriel García Márquez: Writer of Colombia* (London: Cape, 1987), p. 126.

8. Michael Wood, *García Márquez: 'One Hundred Years of Solitude'*, Landmarks of World Literature Series (Cambridge: Cambridge University Press. 1990), p. 78.

9. For an even longer list, see M. Palencia-Roth's 'Gabriel García Márquez; Labyrinths of Love and History', *World Literature Today*, 65,(1991), pp. 54–58 (p. 55).

10. It could be argued that this voyeurism affirms what Luce Irigaray, in her early work *Speculum De l'autre femme* (Paris: Minuit, 1974), calls the 'hommosexual' character of the male gaze. To schematize she characterizes woman as the mirror in which the male observer looks in search of himself, and finds his own phallic image returned to him. Invisible herself, the woman reaffirms this image, guaranteeing the possibility of representation in general and of narrative as one mode of representation.

11. Minta, p. 140. Note also how this coincides with Irigaray's view of men's interest in women as a crucial element in the construction of their own self-image and thus, finally, as self-regarding.

12. See note 5 above.

13. *Love in the Time of Cholera*, trans. by Edith Grossman (Harmondsworth: Penguin, 1989), p. 340.

14. 'The Politics of Ontological Difference', in *Between Feminism and Psychoanalysis*, ed. by Teresa Brennan (London: Routledge, 1989), pp. 89–105 (p. 99).

MICHAEL WOOD

Reading Dazzle

The most casual reader of García Márquez notes his fondness for
numbers. There are one hundred years of solitude, and in the novel of that
name the rain pours down on Macondo for exactly four years, eleven
months, and two days. A traveler circles the earth sixty-five times.
Gargantuan eaters consume for breakfast eight quarts of coffee, thirty raw
eggs, and the juice of forty oranges. The numbers call up an air of legend, a
precision that mildly mocks the idea of precision. But numbers can also
suggest patience, an intimacy with the slow seepage of time. Closer to the
numerical flavor of *Love in the Time of Cholera*, the sad and long-suffering
hero of *No One Writes to the Colonel* (*El coronel no tiene quien le escriba* (1961))
needs, we are told, every counted minute of the seventy-five years of his life
to arrive at the simple word that summarizes both his defeats and his dignity,
his refusal to accept the unacceptable. He is a courteous, old-fashioned man
and has earlier rebuked a group of local youths for swearing. At last, however,
nothing short of rude anger will do. The simple word is shit, *Mierda*.

Love in the Time of Cholera ends on a milder phrase, but one that has
been similarly stored, one that similarly reflects an arithmetic of obstinacy
and concentration. A captain asks how long he can be expected to keep his
boat going up and down a tropical river, and the answer he receives has been

From *Children of Silence: On Contemporary Fiction*. © 1998 Columbia University Press brewing for "fifty-three years, seven months, and eleven days and nights." It is an answer that looks forward as well as backward: "Forever" (*Toda la vida*).

It takes the reader some time to get here too, and on my first reading of this novel I found myself counting pages now and then, the way the characters count years and months. Good stories are best told slowly, Thomas Mann says, but it is possible to have too much of a good thing, and Mann may not be the ideal witness in such a cause. García Márquez really needs the snail's pace he sets, I think, but we need a little patience to understand his need. Or some of us do: the book's huge commercial success suggests that slow telling is making a comeback.

The book begins with a corpse, and the scent of almonds that indicates death by cyanide. "It was inevitable," the doctor thinks who is examining the body, "the scent of bitter almonds always reminded him of the fate of unrequited love." Inevitable, fate, love: we are reading the opening sentence of the book, and we seem already to be deep in an old-fashioned romantic novel. So we are, but we are also caught in the first of García Márquez's narrative lures. What is inevitable is not that deaths by cyanide should be those of lovers but that the doctor should think of such deaths. This one in fact is the first cyanide death he can recall that has nothing to do with love, unrequited or requited. It is not an exception that proves the rule but an unruly event that makes us wonder whether we know what the game is. The doctor himself unfortunately doesn't have much time to wonder, since he dies later the same day in a ridiculous accident, trying to recapture an escaped parrot. And this is the second narrative lure we have already stumbled into. The story we hear at length in the first part of the book is not that of the corpse, as the initial plot moves seem to promise, but that of the doctor and his city and his day. In the rest of the book we hear little more of the corpse or of its earlier life but a great deal more about the doctor, and his wife/widow, and the indefatigable, obsessive fellow who has been in love with her for the amount of time so carefully detailed before the pronunciation of the word "Forever." The corpse is that of Jeremiah de Saint-Amour, an escaped convict turned photographer, who killed himself at the age of sixty because he had decided long ago that he did not want to live beyond that age. Sadly, at the end he found himself regretting his resolve but couldn't think of changing it—"as the date approached he had gradually succumbed to despair as if his death had been not his own decision but an inexorable destiny." This is an important phrase. *Love in the Time of Cholera*, like García Márquez's other novels, is an exploration of destiny, but of this kind of destiny: the kind we invent and displace and fear and desperately live up to or die for.

The setting of the novel is an ancient city on the Caribbean coast of Latin America, the former favorite residence of the viceroys of New

Granada. The city is not named but is a composite picture, García Márquez has said, of Cartagena, Santa Marta, and Baranquilla, places in Colombia where he spent much of his early life. It has a cathedral, a former slave quarter, and a grim colonial building that once housed the inquisition and now (a detail that perhaps nods toward the shade of Buñuel) is occupied by a severely Catholic girls' school. The place resembles Haiti and Cuba because of the sea and the heat and the tropic and the life of the port; it is connected to a colder, mountainous Latin America through its language and its history of empire and independence and civil war. There is much talk of river navigation, of manatees and caimans sporting on the muddy banks of the Magdalena, as well as of ships passing for New Orleans, and of fabulous galleons sunk by English pirates as late as the early eighteenth century. Joseph Conrad is mentioned as involved in an arms deal; the doctor studies in Paris with Dr. Adrien Proust, the father of the novelist. We hear of Dreyfus, the new waltzes of Johann Strauss, the premiere of *The Tales of Hoffman*, the screening of a film called *Cabiria*.

The country is not named either, but it has Colombia's Liberals and Conservatives (the only difference between a Liberal president and a Conservative president, a character says, sounding like Colonel Aureliano Buendia in *One Hundred Years of Solitude*, is that the Liberal is not as well dressed), its War of the Thousand Days, which took place in 1899–1902, and plenty of towns and rivers that would allow us to find our way on an actual map of Colombia. It even anticipates the terrible peacetime violence for which Colombia has become notorious since 1947, a chaotic, wholesale murdering by crooks and guerrillas and the police and the army, a butchery that lacks even the historical shape of a civil war but is none the less real for that. When the Violence (as it is simply, sparely called) was taken to be more or less under control, in 1962 there were still some two hundred civilian deaths occurring each month. It appears here grimly, casually, almost silently, as it does in García Márquez's other books, this time in the shape of corpses floating down river toward the sea, a strange, unaccountable sight, "for there were no more wars or epidemics." Like many other words in this book, and in the historical Latin America it evokes, this clause is both true and deceptive. There are no more epidemics, and we are near the end of the novel. But cholera still exists, even if only endemically, so the time of cholera does continue. There is nothing going on that can really be called a war, unless we insist on the "larval wars that governments were bent on hiding with distracted decrees." But there is random killing, a plague as lethal as any other.

The time of the novel is the later nineteenth and earlier twentieth centuries. A recent event is a showing of the movie *All Quiet on the Western*

Front, which was released in 1939 but may have reached Latin America a little later. More precisely, the present of the novel is just under two years in the 1930s, when all the principal characters are quite old, a lot older than Jeremiah de Saint-Amour, and have no thought of taking his view of things; and there are extensive flashbacks that give us the youth and backgrounds and long lives of these people. The book has been compared to a Naturalist novel and to a photograph album. It's a lot more like the second than like the first, but we might like to pause over the idea of a sophisticated, affectionate Naturalist novel, an evocation of an old, grubby, rigid world for its own sad and charming sake and not for any grim demonstration it might permit. This is a place where an old-fashioned mother can castigate even the contents of her daughter-in-law's sleep: "A decent woman cannot have that kind of dream." The doctor, returning to the city from a long stay in Europe, can hate its filth and its rats and its disease and its backwardness but still love it enough to look at it straight:

> "How noble this city must be," he would say, "for we have spent four hundred years trying to finish it off and we still have not succeeded."

From the paupers' cemetery, one can look down on

> the entire historic city, the broken roofs and the decaying walls, the rubble of fortresses among the brambles, the trail of islands in the bay, the hovels of the poor around the swamps, the immense Caribbean.

This is not a romantic vision, but it is a way one might talk of home.

There is a variety of suspense García Márquez has very much made his own. It consists in giving away conclusions and leaving the reader to guess at how they are reached. The trick characteristically involves removing most of the plausible narrative props, making us dizzily wonder whether already reached conclusions actually can be reached. It is another way of playing with destiny. Liberty creeps into unlikely human spaces, even what has happened seems doubtful, and hindsight, surely the safest of all forms of prophecy, turns risky. Thus we know in this novel that the couple I have just evoked do not marry when young, since we first meet them at the ludicrous death of her husband, the doctor. The suitor is now seventy-six, the woman is seventy-two. He has been waiting, since she first turned him down, for "fifty-one years, nine months, and four days"—a little less than two years short of the final count we have already seen. We learn of their courtship, his numerous affairs, her marriage to the doctor, the doctor's single, scared infidelity, the lovers' happy, belated, foolish reconciliation, old skeletons still able to dance and get frightened at their feelings—though then we are told, in a fine phrase, that they wonder what they are doing "so far from their youth," and that their relation is "beyond love," because it is "beyond the pitfalls of passion, beyond the brutal mockery of hope and the phantoms of disillusion"—*desengaño*, one of those great Spanish words we find both in Baroque poems and lingering as the names of modern streets and lanes, caught up again in an ancient rhetoric of suspicion of the world. What we can't picture, what we must follow page by page, is how any of this can actually come about, how obstacles are removed, how people can bring themselves to say and act as they must to ensure the named developments. García Márquez's formality is impeccable here, a slow joke in its own right. He almost always refers to the doctor by his full name and title, for example: Dr. Juvenal Urbino. His wife invariably appears under her Christian name and maiden name, Fermina Daza; her stubborn lover under his Christian and family name, Florentino Ariza. No modern intimacies of appellation.

The text is not solemn, there are sly gags, fantastic images, and abrupt violences: a group of brothers called after popes (Leon XII, Pius V, and so on); a baby carried around in a bird cage; a woman discovered in adultery and murdered by her husband without a word; a ghost who waves from the river bank; a black doll that silently, eerily grows, becoming too big for its dress and its shoes; a suicide for love (with laudanum, though, another blow to the doctor's theory). But the prose is unruffled, affects not to notice anything untoward. This is a stylistic act, of course, but the chief feature of the act is its discretion. Irony would be too strong a word for the almost invisible humor, the scent of skepticism in the following sentence: "He was a perfect husband: he never picked up anything from the floor, or turned out a light, or closed a door." Such a husband is perfect because there is no chink between him and the myth.

The time of cholera, which is over and not over, is the time of romantic love. Love is like cholera, we are told several times in the book—even its physical symptoms, dizziness, nausea, fever, and the rest, can be the same. Like cholera, love is mortal, exclusive (because it separates us from our world) and undiscriminating (because it doesn't care what kind of victims it gets). García Márquez is fond of telling interviewers that the book he took with him when he first left Colombia for Europe was Defoe's *Journal of the Plague Year*—a story that, apart from doubtless being true, suggests an interest in communities doomed to clinical isolation. The community here is the teeming Caribbean city, not the backland of Macondo, but it is also the community of all those, in Latin America and elsewhere, who are perhaps too keen on morbid metaphors of love. Love is a disease in this book, and this is a romantic novel; but the disease is one of the self-deluding, stubborn will, a fruit of mythology and obstinacy rather than any fate beyond ourselves. Indeed the word itself becomes subject to a kind of creative disintegration or dissemination. At first and most prominently used to evoke the unique, histrionic, weepy passion, the endless topic of soap operas and their predecessors, the kind of the thing that drives people to death through cyanide, it gradually attaches itself to quite various human activities and affections: a long marriage, for example, begun without love, and then finding it and losing it and finding it; the "emergency love," the "hurried love" peddled in brothels; the "loveless love" of desperate people; love for a city, as we have seen; the love of children, love of food, love for life. The first of Florentino Ariza's many mistresses teaches him that "nothing one does in bed is immoral if it helps to perpetuate love." Florentino Ariza himself thinks at one point, "My heart has more rooms than a whorehouse," a secular twist on the rumored many mansions of heaven. The heart: home of sentiment and dream and nostalgia, but also of more erratic, unpredictable emotions, the place where life itself can always turn up and surprise us. Love is the name for attractive and disreputable impulses as well as for all the noble enchantments and illusions, the *engaños* and *encantos* with which we garnish our insufficiently romantic times. If love were always and only a disease, it could only be because life is. Writers have suggested this, but García Márquez is not one of those writers.

In interviews García Márquez has described *Love in the Time of Cholera* not as like a bolero but as "practically a telenovela, a soap opera" and also as a nineteenth-century *feuilleton*, the serial novel that was the soap opera's literary antecedent. It is important to see that García Márquez's novel is not a pastiche of these genres, and still less a parody. It doesn't criticize or condescend to the genres, it seeks, as Stephen Minta has very well said, for "the truths about emotional life which ... are ... solidly embedded in the language of the popular imagination." And yet. The clichés are clichés, however much we may feel at home among them. What are we to do with a discourse that is certainly straight-faced but not entirely straight; something less than ironic; certainly not figurative, indeed devoted to the meticulous reconstruction of a historical world, but still not entirely literal?

There is an answer, I think, suggested chiefly by the behavior of the characters in the novel itself, but first we need to look a little more closely at the stealth of García Márquez's style, and his relation to his soapy sources. There is much discussion of reading in the book, of the doctor's European culture (he is a fan of Loti and Anatole France), of poetry competitions, and above all of the sentimental romances and poems through which so many people conduct so much of their imaginative lives—*versos y folletines de lágrimas*, "verses and tearful serialized love stories." Florentino Ariza immerses himself in books, reads everything from Homer to the lousiest local poets:

> But he made no distinctions: he read whatever came his way, as if it had been ordained by fate, and despite his many years of reading he still could not judge what was good and what was not in all that he read. The only thing clear to him was that he preferred verse to prose, and in verse he preferred love poems.

García Márquez's implication, I take it, is not exactly that this is an ideal reader, but that there are many worse, and that serious, critical readers are often the worst of all.

The language of the book itself, then, is that of fate and broken hearts and eternal passions; of "mists of grief" and the "quicksand" of old age; of a "private hell" and "the wasteland of ... insomnia"; of blood pounding in the veins and "night eternal over the dark sea." Yet the effect, as I have suggested, is neither pastiche nor straight imitation but a form of homage to popular literature, a friendly glance at its often lurid prose. And the prose here is not itself lurid, in spite of the phrases I've just quoted; it is stately, a graceful orchestration of old verbal tunes. What distinguishes this novel from the sentimental work it continuously alludes to is not irony or distance but a certain persistent lucidity. This is not a tearful text; just scrupulously loyal to tearful stories, only occasionally murmuring words such as "fallacy" and "illusion." If it moved faster it would have to judge summarily, settle issues, could hardly avoid the recourse to irony. As it is, time and our patience situate the events and the characters.

Fermina Daza when young, for example, is suddenly sure that what she thought was love is nothing of the kind. She looks at the suitor she has not seen for some time and feels not the passion she has been diligently nurturing but only an "abyss of disenchantment," *desencanto*, another of those great Spanish names for cheated desire. Is she right, or is her disenchantment just ordinary disappointment, of the kind lovers often feel after absences? She is probably wrong, and the text, much later, hints that she is. For the moment, though, she is sure she is right, acts on her feeling, condemns her suitor to a lifetime's despair; more, since she is not a person who can admit mistakes, she will in her own terms always have been right, whatever shifts of feeling may take place in what this novel calls her heart. When García Márquez writes of the "revelation" she experiences, and of the "correctness" of her decision, the words are simple and clear, but several meanings have piled up in them. They point, among other things, to a conviction that alters reality and then takes that alteration as proof of the conviction's justice. A form of destiny. Conversely, Florentino Ariza thinks of himself as doggedly faithful to his one love, in spite of the fact that he has slept with hundreds of other women (he has a note of 622, but there are other affairs too casual to be registered) and even loved some of them. His fidelity is like her certainty, clear to its possessor, questionable to others. By fidelity he means being unable to forget or replace his first love and being able to ensure that news of his apparent infidelities doesn't reach her.

The characters in fact are better guides to meaning than the narrator; better readers of their world and better teachers of reading. Like the characters in García Márquez's earlier novels, indeed like all of us, they are subject to bad luck. We could any of us fall from a ladder and die while trying to rescue a parrot. But they are not, these characters, the victims of fate, prisoners of an author's plot. They write their own lines; they choose their own interpretations of the lines of others; and they are very skillful at both activities.

Florentino Ariza, as a young man of eighteen, brings his first love letter to Fermina Daza. She is sitting sewing outside her house, under the trees, and this is how the occasion is described:

> He took the letter out of his inside jacket pocket and held it before the eyes of the troubled embroiderer, who had still not dared to look at him. She saw the blue envelope trembling in a hand petrified with terror, and she raised the embroidery frame so he could put the letter on it, for she could not admit that she had noticed the trembling of his fingers. Then it happened [*Entonces occurió*]: a bird shook himself among the leaves of the almond trees, and his droppings fell right on the embroidery. Fermina Daza moved the frame out of the way, hid it behind the chair so that he would not notice what had happened [*lo que había pasado*], and looked at him for the first time, her face aflame. Florentino Ariza was impassive as he held the letter in his hand and said, "It's good luck." She thanked him with her first smile and almost snatched the letter away from him.

If this had been a passage in Flaubert, the birdshit would have been a comment on life and love, a sort of visual epigram; if this had been a telenovela, the birdshit wouldn't have appeared at all, would have been edited out or simply not thought of. The interesting point is that Flaubert and the soap opera are in agreement about the incompatibility of birdshit and romance, and García Márquez's narrator, with his ominous narrative signal ("Then it happened") seems ready to feel the same. Until the characters absorb the shit into the romance without breaking step; thereby teaching the narrator, and us, a needed lesson about compatibilities.

Throughout the book we are invited to read language (and the language of gestures) the way the characters do; but I don't know how well we do this. Florentino declares his love to Fermina—his "eternal fidelity and everlasting love," after a fifty-one-year wait—but before he speaks he places his hat over his heart, or more precisely, where his heart is, *en el sitio del corazón*. We can't laugh at the gesture, and we can't patronize him, call him quaint or cute; but we are aware that the gesture itself is empty, an ancient formality rendered moving by the crazy, formless passion that has borrowed its face. Florentino's whole appearance is like this:

> He was what he seemed: a useful and serious old man. His body was bony and erect, his skin dark and clean-shaven, his eyes avid behind round spectacles in silver frames, and he wore a romantic, old fashioned [*un poco tardío para la época*] mustache with waxed tips. He combed the last tufts of his hair at his temples upward and plastered them with brilliantine to the middle of his shining skull as a solution to total baldness. His natural gallantry and languid manner were immediately charming, but they were also considered suspect virtues in a confirmed bachelor. He had spent a great deal of money, ingenuity, and willpower to disguise the seventy-six years he had completed in March, and he was convinced in the solitude of his soul that he had loved in silence for a much longer time than anyone else in this world ever had.

This paragraph ends in a swirl of clichés, which must represent (faithfully, the way Joyce represents Gertie MacDowell's consciousness in the thirteenth chapter of *Ulysses*) Florentino's view of himself. We have in our minds the belated moustache and the unequal fight against baldness. Is this what Romeo would have looked like, if he had lived to seventy-six and moved to Colombia? There is also the odd, uncompromising directness of the paragraph's first sentence: "He was what he seemed to be: a useful and serious old man," *un anciano servicial y serio*. What do we get when we put together the straight talk, the old-fashioned style, the romantic sense of self? Something rather grand, I think, but also something rather oblique, in spite of the direct start. Something like the absurd (but real) grandeur of his claim about being a virgin, which I shall discuss in a moment. We like his style but not on the terms on which that style offers itself. We accept him but not on his valuation. And not, oddly, on the narrator's either, since the narrator's voice becomes a contribution not a summary. This fellow is an *anciano servicial y serio*, sure, but he's also more than that.

The characters take each other seriously but not always literally; they know what clichés mean but can't always say. When Florentino and Fermina get together, at the end of novel, she expresses her surprise that in all the years of their separation—fifty-three years, seven months, eleven days—he has not been known to have a woman, and this in a city where gossip knows everything "even before it's happened." This is too good a chance to miss, a place for the bolero to blossom. "I've remained a virgin for you," Florentino says, *Es que me he conservado virgen para ti*. The likely options for a writer here seem to be the soggy score, a prose of soaring violins, or a knowing wink to the reader: sentimentality or parody. What García Márquez gives us is the character's skepticism. And her belief. And invites in us at the same time a complex implied respect for both characters. Fermina doesn't think this absurd sentence is true, and we know it's not, since we have been told how many women Florentino has slept with, but she likes its style, "the spirited way in which he said it," *el coraje con que lo dijo*.

Fermina is not moved by the thought or the sentiment of the florid claim, although she knows Florentino's emotion to be deep and genuine, in spite of the banality and untruth of the words. She likes the unashamed way in which he assumes the language of romance, the fiction no one believes in, no one needs to believe in, since its function is not to transmit a declared meaning but to allow certain feelings and prowesses to circulate. It is her sense of this function, indeed, which causes Fermina to doubt the truth of Florentino's claim—she doesn't have the information the reader has. "She would not have believed it in any event, even if it had been true, because his love letters were composed of similar phrases whose meaning mattered less than their brilliance," *que no valían por su sentido sino por su poder de deslumbramiento*. Their dazzle. She isn't dazzled, but she likes the dazzle; she can read the dazzle. I think of a remark of Chomsky's in which he expresses surprise that linguists (or anyone) should think of conveying information as the characteristic business of language. "Human language can be used to inform or mislead, to clarify one's own thoughts or to display one's cleverness, or simply for play." And for much else.

The implication here reverses one of modernism's major claims about language and replaces it with something a good deal more optimistic and democratic. Pound quite explicitly and most of the modernists implicitly associate debased or banal language with debased or banal thinking. The kindest option is a sort of uneasy sympathy. When we leaf through the sentimental prose of the Gertie Macdowell chapter of *Ulysses*, we may feel sorry she has no better means of expressing her longings than the trashy idioms of what she reads, we hardly feel at all that she has expressed her longings, still less that these trashy idioms could in any way become an adequate or lively vehicle for them. Yet this is just what García Márquez is proposing, and the move, oddly, brings him close to Henry James, a writer he doesn't mention and perhaps hasn't read. James lends his intelligence to his characters in just the way García Márquez does; not because he has more intelligence but because his intelligence is different and will translate into a more discursive currency. He speaks the reader's language, while the characters speak only their own. Or to put that less obscurely, Fermina doesn't need fancy words, or any words, for her understanding of how language works—she merely needs to know how to act on her understanding. Her understanding is very subtle, however; and so, the suggestion goes, is the understanding of many apparently unsophisticated or unliterary people. The writer needs all the subtlety (and discretion) he/she can muster to get anywhere near it.

There are two kinds of time in García Márquez—at least two. There is the magical, stagnant, modernist time, which scarcely seems to pass; and there is the cumulative, devouring time, which is always passing. Both times are constantly in play—as we see in the famous image of the wheel and the axle in *One Hundred Years of Solitude*, the wheel turning in what looks like cyclical time while the axle wears away according to linear succession—but not always equally accented. We might contrast the time of the Buendias, for example, with the time of the Colonel to whom no one writes.

Love in the Time of Cholera inhabits the Colonel's time but without his despair and ultimate rage. We can't really say that time is accepted here, or that the characters are resigned to it. We have only to think of Florentino's hairdo; of Fermina's wrinkled shoulders, fallen breasts; of these two comically ancient lovers generally, baffled by their renewed romance. Their age is part of what makes them touching, not quite ridiculous but always on the edge of being so—as they themselves quite clearly know. Time is real and regrettable—but not a disaster. Time is the birdshit on the romance, but the romance can accommodate it. It has only to be treated the way many contemporary writers treat clichés—to be treated as the cliché it is. It is possible to make a style out of its banality rather than our despair. If the modernists had been able to do this, their ghosts—Quentin Compson's Southerners, the dictator who doesn't know, even too late, what he is missing, many more—would have been not laid to rest but freed, released from their narrow haunts. Paradise would have been neither lost nor regained but deserted, left to its own devices. It is precisely through this metaphor that Alan Wilde figures the shift from modernism to postmodernism, the second moment releasing, as he puts it, the humanity of the first: "paradise, once lost, is now abandoned." That is, the pathos of loss is abandoned, we make peace with the losses (and gains) of everyday living. In such a view the modernists, staying on, surviving their old anguishes, would have learned the lesson that their anxiety about time hid so thoroughly from them: that we domesticate time, come to terms with it, not by mythifying it but by counting it; not by tearing the hands off our watches, as Quentin Compson does in *The Sound and the Fury*, but by looking steadily at the hands as they go round. And round.

Chronology

1928   Gabriel José García Márquez born on March 6 in Aracataca, Colombia. It is also the year of the banana company massacre, an event Márquez would dwell on at length. His parents are not a presence in his early life. He is reared in the home of his maternal grandfather, Colonel Nicolás Ricardo Márquez Mejía. Gabriel García, García Márquez's father, was considered by the Colonel to be a philanderer, part of the rabble drawn to the banana industry, and of a political bent exactly the opposite of the Colonel. Gabriel García's persistence in the face of the Colonel's low opinion eventually resulted in his marriage to García Márquez's mother, Luisa Santiaga Márquez Iguarán, and the story of their courtship is the inspiration for *Love in the Time of Cholera*. Living in his grandfather's house, García Márquez is surrounded by his aunts. As he tells the literary scholar Plinio Apuleyo Mendoza, the aunts' storytelling and love of the fantastic are shaping forces in García Márquez's writing.

1936   Grandfather dies. García Márquez's grandmother is going blind, so the young man goes to live with his parents in Sucre. His father has found work as a pharmacist. The family has sufficient finances then to send young Gabriel to Barranquilla for primary school.

1940	García Márquez awarded a scholarship to attend secondary school in Zipaquirá.
1946	Graduates secondary school. His first story, "The Third Resignation," published in *El Spectador*.
1947–1949	Studies law at the National University in Bogotá and at the University of Catagena, both in Colombia. Begins journalism career as a reporter for *El Spectador* in Bogotá. Also during this time, reads Kafka's *The Metamorphosis*, translated by Jorge Luis Borges, and is "liberated" at the idea that writing need not follow linear narrative and familiar plots.
1947	Meets Mercedes Barcha Pardo and declares her "the most interesting person" he has ever met. They swear fealty to one another, but will not be married for years.
1950	Leaves law school to pursue journalism full time. Works as a freelancer for several different newspapers and some magazines. Lives in a brothel, begins a number of literary friendships.
1953	Restless and not confident in his writing, García Márquez sells encyclopedias for a short time.
1955	Writes serial installments about a Colombian sailor who survives ten days at sea, the source for what he would later publish as *Story of a Shipwrecked Sailor*.
1955	Sent to Eastern Europe on assignment. Associates of García Márquez send his first book to a publisher. The novella, *Leaf Storm*, is released; it is set in Macondo.
1956	Military shuts down the main paper that employs García Márquez, *El Spectador*. He is trapped in Europe, where he stays for a year. During that time, he writes *No One Writes to the Colonel*. He also tours socialist countries in Europe, intrigued by the possibilities socialism offers for political troubles in Colombia. He sends articles back to newspapers and magazines in Colombia, and also writes *90 Days Behind the Iron Curtain*.
1957	Military regime leaves power in Colombia and García Márquez returns home. He settles in Caracas and writes for *Momento*.
1958	Marries Mercedes Barcha in Barranquilla. He will dedicate the majority of his work to her.
1959	The couple's first son, Rodrigo, is born.

1959–1961	García Márquez works in Cuba, covering the political turmoil in Havana, and briefly in New York. When he moves his family to Mexico City, after resigning his post at *Prensa Latina*, he is denied entrance back into the United States until 1971.
1961	Friends arrange for publication of *No One Writes to the Colonel*.
1962	Friends arrange for publication of *Big Mama's Funeral*. Second son, Gonzalo, is born. *In Evil Hour* also published, but in a heavily edited form which García Márquez rejects. The corrected version will not be published for several years.
1965	Begins work on *One Hundred Years of Solitude*.
1967	*One Hundred Years of Solitude* is published to instant international acclaim, numerous awards, and three years of selling out print runs.
1967	Moves to Barcelona during the last years of the Franco dictatorship.
1972	*Innocent Erendira* published.
1974	Founds *Alternativa*, a leftist newspaper in Bogotá.
1975	Publishes *Autumn of the Patriarch*.
1975–present	Maintains residences in both Mexico City and Bogotá and is active in political causes while founding several civic and political organizations.
1977	Publishes *Operación Carlota*.
1981	Publishes *Chronicle of a Death Foretold*. Wins the French Legion of Honor award.
1982	Wins the Nobel Prize for Literature. Publishes *The Fragrance of Guava*, interviews with Plinio Apuleyo Mendoza.
1985	Publishes *Love in the Time of Cholera*. The book is widely praised, and some critics consider it superior to *One Hundred Years of Solitude*.
1989	Publishes *The General in His Labyrinth*.
1992	Publishes *Strange Pilgrims*, short stories.
1994	Publishes *Love and Other Demons*.
1996	Publishes *News of a Kidnapping*.
2000	García Márquez publicly declares himself "retired."
2002	Publishes a memoir, *Living to Tell the Tale*.

Contributors

HAROLD BLOOM is Sterling Professor of the Humanities at Yale University. He is the author of over 20 books, including *Shelley's Mythmaking* (1959), *The Visionary Company* (1961), *Blake's Apocalypse* (1963), *Yeats* (1970), *A Map of Misreading* (1975), *Kabbalah and Criticism* (1975), *Agon: Toward a Theory of Revisionism* (1982), *The American Religion* (1992), *The Western Canon* (1994), and *Omens of Millennium: The Gnosis of Angels, Dreams, and Resurrection* (1996). *The Anxiety of Influence* (1973) sets forth Professor Bloom's provocative theory of the literary relationships between the great writers and their predecessors. His most recent books include *Shakespeare: The Invention of the Human* (1998), a 1998 National Book Award finalist, *How to Read and Why* (2000), *Genius: A Mosaic of One Hundred Exemplary Creative Minds* (2002), and *Hamlet: Poem Unlimited* (2003). In 1999, Professor Bloom received the prestigious American Academy of Arts and Letters Gold Medal for Criticism, and in 2002 he received the Catalonia International Prize.

RUBÉN PELAYO is Associate Professor of Spanish at Southern Connecticut State University. He is the author of *Gabriel García Márquez: A Critical Companion.*

ROBERTO GONZÁLEZ-ECHEVARRÍA is the Sterling Professor of Spanish at Yale. He is the author of *Myth and Archive: A Theory of Latin American Narrative*; *The Voice of the Masters: Writing and Authority in Modern Latin American Literature*; *Celestina's Brood: Continuities of the Baroque in Spanish and Latin American Literatures*; and many other books.

GENE H. BELL-VILLADA is Professor of Romance Languages at Williams College. He is the author or editor of several books, including *Gabriel Garcia Marquez's One Hundred Years of Solitude: A Casebook; The Pianist Who Liked Ayn Rand: A Novella & 13 Stories*; and *García Márquez: The Man and His Work.*

MICHAEL BELL is Professor of English and Comparative Literature at the University of Warwick, United Kingdom. He is the author of *Gabriel García Márquez: Solitude and Solidarity; Sentimentalism, Ethics and the Culture of Feeling*; and *Literature, Modernity and Myth.*

DAVID BUEHRER is Professor of English at Valdosta State University and the author of articles and scholarly papers on García Márquez, Vargas Llosa Bellow, Fitzgerald, Nabokov, and others.

MABEL MORAÑA is Professor of Latin American Literature at the University of Pittsburgh. She is the author of *Memorias de la generación fantasma* and *Política de la escritura en América Latina, De la Colonia a la Modernidad*, and has edited several collections of criticism. She has also published articles on colonial and contemporary Spanish American literatures and cultural criticism.

JEAN FRANCO, Professor Emeritus of English and Comparative Literature at Columbia University, is an eminent figure in Latin American criticism. She has written extensively on authors such as Rulfo, Cortázar, and Poniatowska. Her books include *Plotting Women: Gender and Representation in Mexico*, *An Introduction to Spanish American Literature*, and *The Decline and Fall of the Lettered City: Latin America in the Cold War.*

M. KEITH BOOKER is Professor of English at the University of Arkansas. He is the author of *Monsters, Mushroom Clouds, and the Cold War: American Science Fiction in Novel and Film, 1946–1964; Film and the American Left: A Research Guide; Critical Essays on Salman Rushdie; The Modern British Novel of the Left: A Research Guide; Colonial Power, Colonial Texts: India in the Modern British Novel*; and several other books.

ANNY BROOKSBANK JONES, Hughes Professor of Spanish at the University of Sheffield, concentrates on Latin American literature and cultural theory, Spanish film and contemporary society. Professor Jones is the co-editor of *Latin American Women's Writing: Feminist Readings in Theory and Crisis* and the author of *women in Contemporary Spain*. She has published

Scholarly essays on Alejandra Pizarnik, María Luisa Bombal, and Norah Lange, among others.

MICHAEL WOOD is class of 1923 Professor of English at Princeton University. His books include studies on Stendhal, on García Márquez, and on Nabokov. He also writes film and literary criticism for the *London Review of Books*, *The New York Review of Books*, *The New York Times Book Review*.

Bibliography

Bell-Villada, Gene H. *García Márquez: The Man and His Work*. Chapel Hill: University of North Carolina Press, 1990.

Beverly, Elizabeth A. The Distance between Bodies. *Commonweal* 115:13 (July 15, 1988): pp. 410–11.

Booker, M. Keith. "The Dangers of Gullible Reading: Narrative as Seduction in García Márquez' *Love in the Time of Cholera*." *Studies in Twentieth Century Literature* 17:2 (Summer 1993): pp. 181–95.

Buehrer, David. "'A Second Chance on Earth': The Postmodern and the Post-Apocalyptic in García Márquez's *Love in the Time of Cholera*." *Critique* 32 (Fall 1990): pp. 15–26.

Columbus, Claudette Kemper. "Faint Echoes and Faded Reflections: Love and Justice in the Time of Cholera." *Twentieth Century Literature* 38 (Spring 1992): pp. 89–100.

Lutes, Todd Oakley. *Shipwreck and Deliverance: Politics, Culture and Modernity in the Works of Octavio Paz, Gabriel García Márquez, and Mario Vargas Llosa*. Lanham: University Press of America, 2003.

Moraña, Mabel. "Modernity and Marginality in *Love in the Time of Cholera*." *Studies in Twentieth Century Literature* 14:1 (Winter 1990): pp. 27–43.

Moyer, Linda Lancione. "Love in the Time of Cholera." *Christianity and Crisis* 48 (September 26, 1988): p. 324.

Oberhelman, Harley D. *García Márquez and Cuba: A Study of its Presence in his Fiction, Journalism, and Cinema*. Fredericton: York Press, 1995.

Palencia-Roth, Michael. "Gabriel García Márquez: Labyrinths of Love and History." *World Literature Today* 65, no. 1 (winter 1991): pp. 54–8.

Pérez, Janet and Wendell Aycock, eds. *Climate and Literature: Reflections of Environment*. Lubbock: Texas Tech University Press, 1995.

Simas, Rosa. *Circularity and Visions of the New World in William Faulkner, Gabriel García Márquez, and Osman Lins*. Lewiston: E. Mellen Press, 1993.

Simpson, Mona. Love Letters. *London Review of Books* 10:15 (September 1, 1988): pp. 22–24.

Acknowledgments

"Love in the Time of Cholera," by Rubén Pelayo, from *Gabriel García Márquez: A Critical Companion*, Westport: Greenwood Press, 2001, pp. 135–161. © 2001 by Rubén Pelayo. Reproduced with permission of Greenwood Publishing Group, Inc., Westport, CT.

"Love in the Golden Years," by Roberto González-Echevarría, from *Yale Review* 78 (Spring 1989): pp. 472–8. © 1989 by Yale University. Reprinted with permission of Yale Review.

"The Novelist of Love," from *García Márquez: The Man and His Work*, by Gene H. Bell-Villada, Chapel Hill: University of North Carolina Press, 1990, pp. 191–202. © 1990 The University of North Carolina Press. Reprinted with permission.

"Not Flaubert's Parrot" from *Gabriel García Márquez: Solitude and Solidarity*, by Michael Bell, New York, St. Martin's Press, 1993, pp. 106–126. © 1993 Michael Bell. Reprinted with permission of the author.

"'A Second Chance on Earth': The Postmodern and The Post-Apocalyptic in García Márquez's *Love in the Time of Cholera*" by David Buehrer, from *Critique* 32 (Fall 1990): pp. 15–26. © 1990 by the Helen Dwight Reid Educational Foundation. Reprinted with permission.

"Modernity and Marginality in *Love in the Time of Cholera*" by Mabel Moraña, from *Studies in Twentieth Century Literature* 14:1 (Winter 1990): pp. 27–43. © 1990 *Studies in Twentieth Century Literature*. Reprinted with permission.

"Dr. Urbino's Parrot" by Jean Franco, from *Indiana Journal of Hispanic Literatures* 1, no. 2 (Spring 1993): pp.147–160. © 1993 by *Indiana Journal of Hispanic Literatures*.

"The Dangers of Gullible Reading: Narrative as Seduction in García Márquez' *Love in the Time of Cholera*" by M. Keith Booker, from *Studies in Twentieth Century Literature* 17:2 (Summer 1993): pp. 181–95. © 1993 *Studies in Twentieth-Century Literature*. Reprinted with permission.

"Utopia and Other Commonplaces in García Márquez's *El amor en los tiempos del cólera*" by Anny Brooksbank Jones, from *The Modern Language Review* 89, part 3 (July 1994): pp. 635–644. © 1994 Modern Humanities Research Association. Reproduced by permission of the publisher and the author.

"Reading Dazzle" from the chapter "Other Times: A Postmodernist Romace (Gabriel García Márquez) in *Children of Silence: On Contemporary Fiction* by Michael Wood, New York: Columbia University Press, 1998, pp. 107–118. © 1998 Columbia University Press.

Index

Characters are alphabetized by their first names.